THE DOUBLE

A Psychoanalytic Study

THE DOUBLE

A Psychoanalytical Study

by OTTO RANK

Translated and Edited,
with an Introduction

by HARRY TUCKER, JR.

Maresfield Library
London 1989

WB

First published in 1971 by
The University of North Carolina Press
Chapel Hill, N.C., U.S.A.
Reprinted 1989 with their permission by
H. Karnac (Books) Ltd
58 Gloucester Road
London SW7 4QY
Reprinted 2000

British Library Cataloguing in Publication Data
Rank, Otto
[*Der Doppelganger*. English]
The Double: A Psychoanalytic Study
Maresfield Library
I. Man. Identity. Psychological Aspects.
I.Title
155.2
ISBN 0 946439 58 3

Printed in Great Britain by Polestar AUP Aberdeen Limited

12/3/04

To Bernhard Blume

Discipulus est prioris posterior dies.
Publilius Syrus, *Sententiae*

PREFACE

Any of us could be the man who encounters his double.[1]

Publication History

A "Der Doppelgänger," in *Imago: Zeitschrift für Anwendung der Psychoanalyse auf die Geisteswissenschaften*, ed. Sigmund Freud. Leipzig, Vienna, and Zürich: Internationaler Psychoanalytischer Verlag, 1914, Vol. III, pp. 97–164.

B "Der Doppelgänger," in Otto Rank, *Psychoanalytische Beiträge zur Mythenforschung: Gesammelte Studien aus den Jahren 1912 bis 1914*. Leipzig and Vienna: Internationaler Psychoanalytischer Verlag, 1919, pp. 267–354.

C *Der Doppelgänger: Eine Psychoanalytische Studie*. Leipzig, Vienna, and Zürich: Internationaler Psychoanalytischer Verlag, 1925, 117 pp.

D *Don Juan. Une étude sur le double*, tr. S. Lautman. Paris: Denoël and Steele, 1932, pp. 9–163.

E "The Double as Immortal Self," in Otto Rank, *Beyond Psychology*. Camden, N.J. Haddon Craftsmen, Inc., 1941, pp. 62–101.

F "The Double as Immortal Self," in Otto Rank, *Beyond Psy-*

---

1. Friedrich Dürrenmatt, "Der Doppelgänger" (Zürich, 1960, Verlags AG "Die Arche"), p. 26.

chology. New York: Dover Publications, Inc., 1958, pp. 62–101.
G *The Double: A Psychoanalytic Study,* tr. and ed. Harry Tucker, Jr. Chapel Hill, N.C.: University of North Carolina Press, 1971.

To summarize briefly, publications A and B are the original article; C is its revision and expansion into a separate publication; D is the translation into French of C (but see below); E is the adaptation of C as a chapter of a posthumous book; F is a second publication of this book; and G is the translation into English of C.

After the publication of A in 1914, the study appeared intact in the first edition of B but not in the second edition (1922), which concentrated more upon mythological essays as such (C, p. 4). C represents the expansion of A (B) into an independent publication which retained part of the material in A (B) and introduced new material presumably accrued since their publication. A detailed presentation of the similarities and differences between A (B) and C was not deemed essential to G, nor are the differences so marked as to be of special concern, except perhaps to the eventual editor of Rank's collected works. D joins Rank's study of the double with his essay on Don Juan, appearing in the publication in that order, despite the title. Here, the five chapters of C are expanded into seven, one of which treats twinship, only briefly mentioned in C. D also provides additional references. An English version of both D and *Don Juan* seems desirable, since both works are complementary; meanwhile, C possesses an interest and significance of its own.

E and F, both of which are identical in word and pagination, are the first English versions of brief and isolated parts of C. Although the posthumous publications E (F) may be taken as Rank's final words on the subject of the double, a reading of the 1925 book (C) is desirable for a complete understanding, especially since E (F) omit much that appeared in C (e.g., the detailed description of *The Student of Prague*). Readers having an interest in Rank himself, as well as in the motif of the double, will need to know not only E (F), but also C itself, D, or G. In part, the relationship of E (F) to C resembles that of C to A and B: portions of E (F) are taken verbatim from C (e.g., E, F, p. 80; cf. C, pp. 64–65); yet in E (F) there is additional material which came to the author's subsequent notice (e.g., E, F, pp. 78, 79, 85, and *passim*). Otherwise, the principle difference between

E (*F*) and *C* is one of scope and emphasis: where *C* was concerned primarily with clarifying the literary, psychoanalytic, mythical, and ethnological meanings of the double, *E* (*F*) correlate the motif with Rank's ideas of the artist and the hero (see Introduction, p. xvi) *E* (*F*) do not reveal any substantial changes in the conclusions which the author reached in *C;* and, at this writing, *D* and *G* are the only translations of this final German version.

The Translation (*G*)

The translation attempts to adhere closely to the meaning of Rank's sentences *pari passu* and to express this meaning in a style acceptable to the reader. Departures from the literal text were made to provide a felicitous English rendering, but care was taken that this rendering did not distort the thought expressed in German. The translation, then, endeavors to avoid the opposite pitfalls of being too "free" or of remaining so near to the original that the result would have been objectionable English. If the translation has generally been successful in steering a middle course, it will have accomplished its linguistic purpose. Here and there, the Germanic flavor may well be apparent; but since this flavor ultimately is that of the author rather than of the translator, it may perhaps not inappropriately remain.

Rank depended in rather large measure upon German translations of authors whose works in the original language were either unavailable to him or with whom he was unfamiliar in the original. Except for the quotations from Coleridge, Kipling, Poe, Stevenson, and Wilde, reference to whose works in the original is given, I proceeded on the assumption that reliance could be placed both upon the accuracy of Rank's citations and upon the accuracy of the German translations themselves (e.g., S. Lipiner's translation of Mieciewicz' *Diadys,* and Carl von Gütschow's translation of Merezhkovsky's *Tolstoy and Dostoyevsky*). Although it may be true that a thorough investigation of Rank's sources would examine and compare these originals and their versions in other languages, it seemed that such documentation was not suitable to the purpose of this translation, which intends to present Rank's book in English substantially as it appeared in 1925. I have followed this procedure also in his quotations from German authors, which I have checked *passim.*

The question of whether to translate the titles of the primary and secondary sources, or to leave them in the original, seemed best answered by following the general procedure of translating them in the body of the text and leaving their original titles as the notes cite them. This method appeared to serve the needs of both the specialist and the general reader: the former will expect to have the bibliographical information, while the latter ordinarily will not be concerned with detailed documentation. In this way the translation intends to appeal, as did the original, not only to a professional audience but also to the educated layman.

Certain footnotes were omitted since they have little or no interest for those whose primary language is English. These include references to German translations of works in English (e.g., to an edition of Poe's stories), the originals of which are readily accessible. Otherwise, Rank's notes appear substantially as he wrote them.

‧ In the text and notes I have supplied, when available, those citations which the original did not provide. Brackets enclose editorial material, and references are given for translations other than mine.

I express my warm thanks to those who, in one way or another, have encouraged this publication and assisted with the many problems which arose: Mr. Lambert Davis, former Director of The University of North Carolina Press, without whose patient and knowledgeable help the project would not have matured; Professor Norman N. Holland of the State University of New York at Buffalo; Professor Ralph V. Tymms of Royal Holloway College (University of London); Professor E. William Rollins, Mr. Gifford S. Nickerson, and Mr. James L. Ivey, all of North Carolina State University; Wilmer C. Betts, M.D.; Mrs. Harold L. Bello; S.S.; and my wife, who has cheerfully coped with the problems posed by a husband often preoccupied, as Friedrich Raimund put it, with "the damned carryings-on with doubles."

HARRY TUCKER, JR.
North Carolina State University at Raleigh

CONTENTS

INTRODUCTION

The more you press towards the heart of a narrowly bounded historical problem, the more likely you are to encounter in the problem itself a pressure which drives you outward beyond those bounds.[1]

The critics and literary historians of the nineteenth century, that century which saw the inception and progressive development of scholarship as we know it today, were not able to penetrate beyond a surface interpretation of the portrayal of doubles in literature. Having noted it as a technique in comedy, they went on to ascribe its use in prose fiction generally to the predilection of the author for the unreal and uncanny, to his desire to depict distinct and separate traits of himself, or to his desire for another existence. The prominent Germanist Richard M. Meyer was writing in this tradition in 1916 when he described E. T. A. Hoffmann's use of the double-theme as arising from his "longing for a more exalted existence." Meyer stated too that the doubles themselves, "unsure of their identity, are sometimes inhabitants of this earth and sometimes belong to some unearthly region."[2] It remained for psychoanalysis, with both its clinical and

1. Arthur O. Lovejoy, *Essays in the History of Ideas* (Baltimore, 1948), p. 6.
2. Richard M. Meyer, *Die deutsche Literatur bis zum Beginn des neunzehnten Jahrhunderts* (Berlin, 1916), p. 630. Although Meyer does admit here that the double may be interpreted as a figure from the past, as does Rank (see p. 6), the reference is casual and carried no further.

cultural interests, to examine this motif in terms of depth psychology and myth and to relate its use more clearly to the authors themselves (in the wake of Wilhelm Dilthey). Such examination demonstrated that this use of the double-theme derived not so much from the authors' conscious fondness for describing preternatural situations (Hoffmann), or separate parts of their personalities (Jean Paul), as from their unconscious impulse to lend imagery to a universal human problem—that of the relation of the self to the self. Since Emil Lucka's paper "Duplications of the Self" ("Verdoppelungen des Ich," 1904) dealt with this problem largely from a philosophical standpoint, Otto Rank's book (1925) and *Doubles in Literary Psychology* (1949) by Ralph Tymms have remained the only attempts, exclusive of studies more restricted in scope, to consider the double as it appears in poetry, drama, and prose fiction. As such, of course, these works are significant contributions to the scholarship of comparative literature, a discipline which did not attain maturity until the first half of this century.

The Double and *Doubles in Literary Psychology*

Since Rank and Tymms investigated essentially the same topic, a brief description of the similarities and differences in their monographs is in order. Rank, the real pioneer, apparently found the impetus for his work in a motion picture of his day, *The Student of Prague*, which prompted him to study the literary, psychological, mythical, and ethnological sources and illustrations of the double. (It is certainly true, as Richard D. Altick has abundantly shown in *The Scholar Adventurers* [New York, 1966], that incidents inconsequential in themselves can sometimes lead to scholarly results of the first magnitude.) Rank was particularly well-equipped for his task by virtue of his degree in Germanics from Vienna (1912). In a sense, then, he was breaking ground for Professor Tymms, who indeed acknowledges his indebtedness to the Austrian psychoanalyst and first lay analyst (*Doubles in Literary Psychology*, pp. 40–41, n.).

Where Rank's approach is preponderantly heuristic, psychoanalytical, and theoretical, that of Tymms is literary and historical; where Rank's presentation, though not diffuse, is not very tightly organized either, that of Tymms takes up successively "The Origin and Development of the Double"; "The Double, or Doppelgänger, in German Romantic Literature"; and "The Double in Post-Romantic Literature." In fact, Tymms' Table of Contents appears as a step-by-step outline of his entire discussion. Both authors reveal a knowledge, extensive in breadth and depth, of the literature of the Western world, although Tymms provides more examples than does Rank since he draws upon those sources which appeared between 1925 and 1949. Tymms expresses his reaction to Rank's work as follows:

[Rank] bases his interpretation of the whole theme of the double on the Freudian theory of Narcissism [sic]. According to this view, the double represents elements of morbid self-love which prevent the formation of a happily balanced personality. (Convincing as this theory may be as an explanation of Schlemihl, possibly of Hoffmann's Elixiere, and certainly of Wilde's Dorian Gray, it surely applies less well to several other examples of the theme: Chamisso's "Erscheinung," for instance, in which the double represents the precise counterpart, or antidote, to this element of self-love.)[3]

Tymms himself presents the double as an allegorical representation or as a projection of the second self of the unconscious (pp. 119 ff.). Unlike Rank, he refers especially to the influence of German Romantic psychology, particularly to that of Franz Anton Mesmer (pp. 26 f.; pp. 35 ff.). In sum, Rank writes as a psychoanalyst and Tymms as a literary historian; Rank's approach is inductive, while that of Tymms is deductive; Rank leans heavily on anthropological evidence, while to Tymms it seems of secondary importance; and, because of the restrictive nature of the topic, both studies deal with the same literary works. It cannot be said, however, that Doubles in Literary Psychology supersedes Rank's essay in any sense, nor does it make this claim. Its considerable merit is that it carried forward, and exhaustively so, the thematic investigation which Otto Rank undertook, adducing and discussing material supplementary to that of Rank. In fine, both books are separate, yet linked, expositions which are indispensable to any further examination of the occurrence of the double-motif in Western literature and culture, or possibly elsewhere.

3. Ralph Tymms, Doubles in Literary Psychology (Cambridge, England, 1949), pp. 40–41. In "Erscheinung" Chamisso describes his double as being an antagonist, a description which seems to accord quite well with Rank's idea of the double as often personifying the "bad," or threatening, self (e.g., in The Student of Prague and in Maupassant's La Horla). In a communication to me of 28 March 1970, Professor Tymms admits the possibility of this interpretation but believes that the passage quoted above still offers the more probable point of view.

Der Doppelgänger and "The Double as Immortal Self"

During the closing years of his life, Otto Rank decided that his study of the double, which had appeared on four separate occasions, should receive further attention. "The subject of the Double still does interest me and I shall probably like to go back to it once more," he writes in a letter to Jessie Taft.[4] Where *Der Doppelgänger: Eine Psychoanalytische Studie* (*C*) concentrated upon explaining the occurrence of the motif in psychological, ethnological, mythical, and literary terms,[5] "The Double as Immortal Self" (*E[F]*), the second chapter of *Beyond Psychology* (posthumous), presents the theme in relation to his much earlier works, *Der Künstler: Ansätze zu einer Sexual-Psychologie* (Vienna, 1907; *Art and Artist*, New York, 1932), and *Der Mythus von der Geburt des Helden* (Vienna, 1909; *The Myth of the Birth of the Hero*, New York, 1914). In *E(F)*, Rank posits that man's need for self-perpetuation, for immortalizing himself, led to the development of civilization and its spiritual values (pp. 62–65). The primitive concept of the soul as a duality (the person and his shadow) appears in modern man in the motif of the double, assuring him, on the one hand, of immortality and, on the other, threateningly announcing his death (pp. 73–76). Rank holds that the main distinction of the artist, in contrast to the neurotic individual, is the artist's ability ". . . to present his creation in an acceptable form justifying the survival of the irrational in the midst of our over-rationalized civilization" (p. 77), thus giving a rational form to the irrational both in himself and in folk-belief (p. 83). The remainder of *E(F)* calls attention to twinship as the earliest manifestation of the "Double-soul" (pp. 84–92), to the hero as embodying both the mortal and the immortal self (pp. 93–96), and to the artist as being the hero's "spiritual double," thus assuring himself of immortality in his art (pp. 97–101). At the same time, the double points up ". . . man's eternal conflict with himself and others, the struggle between his need for likeness and his desire for difference" (p. 99), a conflict which leads to the creation of a spiritual double in favor of self-perpetuation and in abnegation of the physical double which signifies mortality (pp. 99–100).

While *E(F)* thus represent significant advances in Rank's

---

4. Jessie Taft, *Otto Rank* (New York, 1958), p. 212.
5. See the Preface for Rank's treatments of the subject.

thinking on the double, and, indeed, may be taken as his last word on the subject, C is the foundation upon which he built these advances and must be taken into account by the reader of E or F. The main difference between C and $E(F)$ lies not so much in Rank's breach with orthodox Freudian views after 1924, as in his application of his former studies to a renewed examination of the subject. It is quite conceivable that, had he lived to read it, Sigmund Freud, with his constant interest in the typological applications of the psychoanalysis which he founded, could have given his approval to "The Double as Immortal Self."

The Use of Anthropology in *The Double*[6]

As the motto to *The Interpretation of Dreams*, Freud chose Vergil's statement, "Flectere si nequeo Superos, Acheronta movebo" ("If I am unable to move the gods above, then I shall stir up those in the nether world"). From its beginning, however, psychoanalysis might well have been characterized by the "Homo sum; humani nihil a me alienum puto" of Terence ("I am a human being; and so I believe that nothing human is foreign to me"). Having started as an exploration into the mental life of the individual patient, psychoanalysis turned, especially after the establishment of its professional journals, to the application of its principles to civilized society both present and past; nor did it neglect those less civilized social groups which had been, or were in the process of being, studied by anthropology. As a separate discipline, this field of study did not by very much antedate psychoanalysis itself. (The impetus to modern anthropology was provided by Darwin's *On the Origin of Species* [1859], appearing three years after Freud's birth.) Of the early analysts, Otto Rank, Geza Róheim, and Theodor Reik contributed significantly to correlations of the new psychoanalytic theories with the observations gained by students of anthropology and ethnology. We are concerned here with those observations only in the measure that Rank used them in Chapter IV, which documents anthropological evidence in support of his interpretations of the double.

The sources which Rank cites in Chapter IV (Frazer, Tylor, Bastian, and others) represent the "armchair speculation" which characterized Old World evolutionary anthropology. By 1914,

---

6. For a critical reading of Chapter IV and for assistance in writing this section I am indebted to Mr. Gifford S. Nickerson of the Department of Sociology and Anthropology at North Carolina State University.

the year of the first appearance of his essay, a significant number of anthropologists, notably in England (Reginald Radcliffe-Brown, Bronislaw Malinowski) and North America (Franz Boas) had moved away from the traditional view of "primitive" peoples as "fossilized" cultures (somewhat as archetypes of prehistoric man). They turned to empirical field research, which showed that, far from being immutable and everywhere the same, certain beliefs and superstitions do undergo alterations within individual cultures. Present-day anthropology, therefore, would be unable to accept the generalizations which Rank draws from isolated instances; nor would Chapter IV's presentation of the guardian spirit be acceptable. Rank was evidently unaware that the North American Indians generally never thought of such spirits as being harmful and, with the exception of the Southwest Pueblo cultures, did not anthropomorphize them.

It would hardly be fair, however, to dismiss Chapter IV outright because of such dated anthropological views, since Rank was using what sources he had at hand—sources which, particularly in Central Europe, tended to adhere to the evolutionary approach. For this reason, too, it is understandable that his readers, even in 1925, would have had few objections to his conclusions, since by that time Frazer's influence and methodology were still felt by many European anthropologists.

It should also be pointed out that the relationship which Rank assumes to exist between paranoia and homosexuality (see Chapter V) appears today to be no longer tenable. The discussion of this question, however, lies outside the scope of this publication.

The Reception of *The Double*

Five years after its appearance in *Imago*, Rank's paper was abstracted at length by Louise Brink in *The Psychoanalytic Review*, VI (1919), 450–60. As a book, however, it seems only to have drawn the attention of Erich Stern.

Again and again the theme of the double recurs in literature: we find it in E. T. A. Hoffmann, Hans [*sic*] Heinz Ewers, Chamisso, Andersen, Dostoyevsky, Jean Paul, Oscar Wilde, and others. In adducing the insights gained by psychoanalysis, Rank seeks to make this double-motif comprehensible, in which task he points to its frequent occurrences at more primitive levels of culture, and, concurrently, to the significance which it there assumes. It appears as an effluence of narcissistic ties, of self-infatuation, which, just as in the child, plays a large role among primitive peoples, and which we also see in the neurotic individual. The hero's consciousness of his guilt causes him to transfer the responsibility for certain deeds of the self to another self, the double; his tremendous fear of death leads to a transference to the double. In order to escape this fear of death, the person resorts to suicide which, however, he carries out on his double, because he loves and esteems his ego so very much. And finally, the double represents the embodiment of the soul. The interesting monograph shows the significance of psychoanalysis for the understanding of literary creations.[7]

Possible reasons for the apparent lack of attention from Rank's peers are that the study had already appeared twice ($A[B]$) and that *The Trauma of Birth* in the previous year had estranged Rank from the orthodox psychoanalytic camp, thus perhaps rendering his further publications unworthy of concern to the loyal followers of Freud. Nor, at that time, could it be expected that those non-German periodicals concerned with the academic study of literature would pay much heed to an essay which interpreted a literary theme from the viewpoint of psychoanalysis. In the United States, for example, the academic approach to literary work was generally pedestrian, traditional, and undisposed to accept psychological criticism. It was to be some time before scholars in general realized that "to 'read' an author, in any but a superficial and mechanical manner, is to be aware of the import of the idea which he is expressing in each passage and of the *relations* (not always explicit, often even *unconscious* [emphasis mine]) of the ideas in one passage to those in another, whether they be relations of simple congruity or mutual implication or mutual incongruity; and to be constantly observant of the transitions from one strain of thought to another."[8]

The Double and Society

It is noteworthy that the interest of the reading (and listening) public seems especially to have been drawn to the theme of the double during or just after major upheavals of society. So Jean Paul's *Siebenkäs* (1796) and *Titan* (1800) appeared in a Germany fragmented by Napoleon's hegemony; Chamisso (himself divided between France and Germany) began his *Peter Schlemihls wundersame Geschichte* in the year of the Battle of Leipzig, 1813, and published it in 1814; Hoffmann's *Die Elixiere des Teufels* appeared in the year of Waterloo, 1815; Hofmannsthal's

7. Erich Stern, review of Otto Rank's *Der Doppelgänger*, in *Die Literatur*, XXIX (1926–1927), 555.

8. Arthur O. Lovejoy, *Essays in the History of Ideas* (Baltimore, 1948), p. xvi.

Die Frau ohne Schatten appeared the year after the close of World War I; Werfel's *Spiegelmensch* came out the following year in a country approaching inflation; and Dürrenmatt's *Der Doppelgänger* was heard a year after the end of World War II. Should it be pointed out that Dürrenmatt, a Swiss, had no active part in Europe's collapse, the reminder only forms a part of the questions posed: is there some relationship between extensive disruptions of society, with their concomitant unsettling effects upon the individual, and the interest of the literate public in descriptions of doubles imaginatively portrayed? If such a relationship does obtain, what is its nature? Only skilled and cautious investigation can provide answers to these questions—investigation which should heed the conclusions reached in Rank's and Tymms' books as well as the information provided by political and social history, comparative literature, literary criticism, and psychology, to name only five areas which should be involved in such a study.

We can, however, approach the problem by observing that either negative or positive answers seem possible. (1) There is no causal relationship between social upheavals and the concurrent or subsequent use by writers of the double-motif since, if there were such a relationship, this motif would have appeared much more frequently than it has and would have attracted many more readers over a longer period of time. Further, there have been periods of social disorganization or reorganization (e.g., the Thirty Years' War) in which the theme of the double either did not appear or was insignificant. (2) Psychology, as we know it today, had its beginnings at the end of the eighteenth century and in the nineteenth. The quest into the mind is simultaneously the quest into the individuality and integrity of the self, which can exhibit puzzling contradictions and obscurely understood drives and impulses. It is not surprising, then, that the theme of the double prominently appeared just when introspective German Romanticism was nascent, and that it continued to appear along with the development of psychology into an independent discipline. Major wars and other extensive disturbances of society are among those occasions which cause man to ask himself fundamental questions about his identity—an identity which he finds existing on various levels or even in fragmentation. This questioning of one's identity has, since Kant, become more and more part of the human problem; and so it seems quite in accord with this confrontation of man with himself that the use of the double-motif appeared in the time of Napoleon and Fichte and has continued into the near present.

These are, of course, only speculations; and it is to be hoped that a careful and intensive study of the problem will provide reasonably acceptable answers.

Conclusion

Along with the questions raised in the preceding section, one may also note that the subject of the double, in all its literary and psychological manifestations, has not yet found the sufficiently searching and up-to-date study that it deserves. Such a study might most feasibly be collaborative between the disciplines of comparative literature, anthropology, and clinical psychology (subsuming psychoanalysis and psychiatry). Symposia on the topic might well initiate such a project, the result of which could be a comprehensive report and survey valuable to the humanist and scientist alike. To suggest that some correlation might possibly appear between literary and clinical instances, the bibliography here appended includes references to the nosological entity of autoscopia. Is there a relationship between writing about doubles and perceiving them proprioceptively? If so, what is the nature of this relationship? Surely those of us engaged in the study and teaching of imaginative literature ought to learn from the knowledge and research of our colleagues in the scientific disciplines.[9]

Of those who comprised the "circle around Freud" between 1904 and 1924, Otto Rank was the one who applied the new psychoanalysis most extensively and diligently not only to patients (as mentioned previously, he was the first lay analyst), but also to various facets of culture. His monumental study, *Incest in Literature and Legend: Fundamentals Toward a Psychology of Literary Creativity* (*Das Inzest-Motiv in Dichtung und Sage: Grundzüge einer Psychologie des dichterischen Schaffens* [Vienna, 1912; 2nd ed., 1926]), not yet translated into English, is

9. These colleagues perhaps could provide an explanation for the interesting feature, already noted by Otto Weininger, that the double does not appear in the female, but solely in the male form (see Emil Lucka, "Verdoppelungen des Ich," *Preussische Jahrbücher*, CXV (1904), 59, n.). Lovejoy also states that ". . . there is imperative need of more definite, responsible, organized collaboration between specialists in these several branches [of knowledge] than has hitherto been customary—collaboration too, in some cases, between historians and specialists in nonhistorical disciplines, notably the natural sciences" (p. 10).

doubtlessly the most convincing evidence of his strong interest in the relationships between literature and psychology, also shown in *The Double* and other publications. The study of these relationships happily continues in our country in the existence of *American Imago, Literature and Psychology,* The Otto Rank Association, the Association for Applied Psychoanalysis, and in the publications of individual scholars and clinicians.

Bibliography

COLEMAN, STANLEY M. "The Phantom Double," *British Journal of Medical Psychology,* XIV (1934), 254–73.

DOWNEY, J. E. "Literary Self-Projection," *Psychological Review,* XIX (July, 1912), 299–311.

DÜRRENMATT, FRIEDRICH. "Der Doppelgänger," in *Gesammelte Hörspiele.* Zürich, 1960, pp. 7–37.

EISENSTEIN, SAMUEL. "Otto Rank: The Myth of the Birth of the Hero," in *Psychoanalytic Pioneers,* ed. Franz Alexander *et al.* New York and London, 1966, pp. 36–50.

HESSEN, H., and GREEN, A. "Sur l'héautoscopie," *Encephale,* XLVI (1957), 581–94.

LHERMITTE, JEAN. "De l'image corporelle et ses déformations morbides," *J. Psych. norm. Path.,* XXXVII–XXXVIII (1940–1941), 321–45.

LUCKA, EMIL. "Verdoppelungen des Ich," *Preussische Jahrbücher,* CXV (1904), 54–83.

LUKIANOWICZ, N. "Autoscopic Phenomena," *A. M. A. Arch. Neurol. Psychiat.,* LXXX (1958), 199–220. Contains 101 references.

MENNINGER-LERCHENTHAL, E. "Der eigene Doppelgänger," *Psychotherapeutische Praxis,* III (1937), 143–94.

———. "Der eigene Doppelgänger," *Schweizer Zt. Psychol.,* suppl. 11 (1946), 96 pp.

REBER, NATALIE. "Studien zum Motiv des Doppelgängers bei Dostojevskij und bei E. T. A. Hoffmann," in *Osteuropastudien der Hochschulen des Landes Hessen, Reihe II, Marburger Abhandlungen zur Geschichte und Kultur Osteuropas,* Vol. VI. Giessen: Im Kommissionsverlag Wilhelm Schmitz, 1964. This reference was kindly provided by Professor Tymms.

SCHMITT, FRANZ A. *Stoff- und Motivgeschichte der deutschen Literatur: eine Bibliographie.* Berlin, 1965, p. 46.

TAFT, JESSIE. *Otto Rank.* New York, 1958.

TYMMS, RALPH. *Doubles in Literary Psychology.* Cambridge, England, 1949; bibliography, pp. 122–26.

VINGE, LOUISE. *The Narcissus Theme in Western European Literature up to the Early Nineteenth Century.* Lund, 1967.

THE DOUBLE

A Psychoanalytic Study

I

The Statement
of the Problem

Wheresoe'er toward sleep I turned,
Wheresoe'er for death I yearned,
Wheresoe'er I trod the ground,
On my way sat down by me
A wretched wight, black-vestured he,
In whom a brother's guise I found.

MUSSET

The technique of psychoanalysis generally aims at uncovering deeply buried and significant psychic material, on occasion proceeding from the manifest surface evidence. Psychoanalysis need not shy away even from some random and banal subject, if the matter at hand exhibits psychological problems whose sources and implications are not obvious. There should be no objection, then, if we take as a point of departure a "romantic drama," which not long ago made the rounds of our cinemas. We can thus trace back the developmental and semantic history of an old, traditional folk-concept which has stimulated imaginative and thoughtful writers to use it in their works. Those whose concern is with literature may be reassured by the fact that the scenarist of this film, *The Student of Prague*, is an author currently in vogue and that he has adhered to prominent patterns, the effectiveness of which has been tested by time.

Any apprehensions about the real value of a photoplay which aims so largely at achieving external effects may be postponed until we have seen in what sense a subject based upon an ancient folk-tradition, and the content of which is so eminently psychological, is altered by the demands of modern techniques of expression. It may perhaps turn out that cinematography, which in numerous ways reminds us of the dream-work, can also express certain psychological facts and relationships—which the writer often is unable to describe with verbal clarity—in such clear and conspicuous imagery that it facilitates our understanding of them. The film attracts our attention all the more readily since we have learned from similar studies that a modern treatment is often successful in reapproaching, intuitively, the real meaning of an ancient theme which has become either unintelligible or misunderstood in its course through tradition.[1]

First of all, let us try to capture the shadowy, fleeting, but impressive scenes of the film-drama by Hans [*sic*] Heinz Ewers:

Balduin, the most dashing student and the best fencer at the University of Prague, has dissipated all his money and is weary of his profligate activities. Crossly, he turns aside from his cronies and their diversion with the dancer Lyduschka. Then a sinister old man, Scapinelli, approaches him and offers help. Roaming through the forest and conversing with this strange adventurer, Balduin witnesses a hunting accident of the Count von Schwarzenberg's young daughter, whom he rescues from drowning. He is invited to her castle, where he meets her cousin and fiancé, Baron Waldis-Schwarzenberg. Although he behaves awkwardly and has to leave in discomfiture, he has made such an impression upon the count's daughter that, from then on, she indicates frostily to her fiancé that he should keep his distance.

At his lodgings Balduin practices fencing positions in front of his large mirror and then falls into disconsolate reflections about his unpleasant situation. Scapinelli appears and offers him wealth upon the signing of a contract that will permit Scapinelli to take from Balduin's room whatever he pleases. Balduin laughs, points to the bare walls and primitive furnishings, and happily signs the document. Scapinelli looks inquisitively about the room, apparently finding nothing that will suit him, until he finally points to Balduin's *mirror-image*. The student willingly goes along with the supposed joke but is numbed with astonishment when he sees his *alter ego* detach itself

---

1. See Otto Rank, *Die Don-Juan-Gestalt* (Vienna, 1924).

from the mirror and follow the old man through the door and out upon the street.

Now an elegant gentleman, the former impoverished student has gained entry into circles where he again sees the much-admired count's daughter. At a ball he has the chance to confess his love to her on the castle terrace. This moonlit idyl, however, is interrupted by her fiancé and is overheard by Lyduschka, who now crosses Balduin's path as a flower girl and follows him incessantly on perilous roads. Balduin is abruptly torn away from the sweet thoughts of the first success of his suit by the apparition of his reflection which, leaning against a column, appears on the parapet of the veranda. Believing that his eyes have deceived him, he is jolted from semiconsciousness only by the approach of his friends. As he departs, Balduin slips a note into his beloved's handkerchief, which she had dropped; the note asks her to come to the Hebrew cemetery the next night. Lyduschka furtively follows the count's daughter to her room in order to learn the contents of the note; but she finds only the handkerchief and Balduin's stickpin, which he had used as a fastener.

On the next evening the princess [*sic*] hurries to the rendezvous; Lyduschka, who sees her by chance, follows her like a shadow. In the deserted cemetery the lovers stroll in the splendid moonlight. They pause atop a small knoll, and Balduin is just about to kiss his beloved for the first time when he stops short, staring horrified at his double who has suddenly revealed himself behind one of the headstones. While Margit flees in terror of the uncanny apparition, Balduin vainly tries to capture his likeness, who has disappeared just as suddenly as he came.

Meanwhile, Lyduschka has taken the handkerchief and Balduin's tiepin to Margit's fiancé, who decides to challenge Balduin to a duel with sabers. Since Waldis-Schwarzenberg pays no heed to the warnings of Balduin's skill in fencing, the old Count Schwarzenberg, who is already indebted to Balduin for the rescue of his daughter, decides to ask that the life of his future son-in-law, and only heir, be spared. With some reluctance Balduin gives his word not to slay his opponent. But in the forest on the way to the duel, his earlier self comes toward him, holding a bloody saber and wiping it clean. Even before Balduin comes to the spot where the duel is to take place, he sees from a distance that his other self has already slain his opponent.

His desperation increases still more when, from now on, he is no longer admitted into the count's house. He makes a futile attempt to forget his love in wine; while playing cards, he sees his double opposite him; and Lyduschka entices him, but with no success. He must see his beloved again; and one night—on the same path which Lyduschka earlier had used—Balduin sneaks into the room of Margit, who has not yet forgotten him. Sobbing, he casts himself at her feet. She forgives him and their lips meet in the first kiss. Then, at an accidental movement, she notices in the mirror that his image is not reflected next to hers. Terrified, she asks the reason, and he covers his head in shame as his mirror-image appears grinning at the door.

Margit swoons at the sight, and Balduin escapes in terror, followed at every step by the gruesome shadow. So pursued, he flees through the streets and alleyways, over walls and ditches, through meadow and forest. Finally, he comes upon a carriage, throws himself into it, and urges the coachman to the greatest possible speed. After a rather long drive at a furious pace, Balduin believes that he is safe, gets out, and is about to pay the coachman, when he recognizes his reflection in the man. In frenzy he rushes on. He sees the spectral figure on all street-corners and must plunge past it into his house, where he securely locks all the doors and windows.

On the point of putting an end to his life, he places his loaded pistol in readiness and prepares to write down his last will and testament. But again, his double stands grinning before him. Bereft of all control over his senses, Balduin seizes the weapon and fires at the phantom, which disappears at once. He laughs with relief and, believing that he is now rid of all torments, uncovers his hand-mirror —formerly wrapped carefully with cloth—and views himself for the first time in a long while. In that same moment he feels a keen pain in the left part of his chest, is aware that his shirt is soaked with blood, and realizes that he has been shot. In the next instant he collapses to the floor, dead. The smirking Scapinelli appears, in order to tear up the contract over the corpse.

The last scene shows Balduin's grave beside a body of water, shaded by a huge weeping willow. His double is sitting on the mound of the grave with the uncanny black bird [raven?], the constant companion of Scapinelli. The beautiful verses of Musset ("December Night") elucidate:

> Wherever you go, I shall be there always,
> Up to the very last one of your days,
> When I shall go to sit on your stone.

The scenario does not leave us long in doubt about the intention and meaning of these uncanny happenings. The "basic idea" is supposed to be that a person's past inescapably clings to him and that it becomes his fate as soon as he tries to get rid of it. This past life is meant to be embodied in Balduin's reflection and also in the enigmatic character of Lyduschka, who pursues him from his former life as a student. It may be that this attempt at an explanation—rather than stressing the basic idea inherent in the subject itself—may in certain respects be sufficient; but certainly this allegorical interpretation is unable either to plumb the content of the film or to justify fully the lively impression of its plot. For there remain enough striking features in it which require explanation—above all, the facts that the eerie double must disturb only "all hours of sweet company" of the couple, and that he becomes visible only to them. Actually, his interventions become more terrifying in proportion as the demonstrations of their love become more fervent. At Balduin's avowal of love on the terrace, his mirror-image appears, so to speak, as a silent figure of warning; at the meeting of the lovers at night in the cemetery, he interrupts their growing intimacy by preventing their first kiss; and finally, in the decisive meeting of reconciliation, which is sealed by an embrace and a kiss, he forcefully separates the lovers forever. So the hero really turns out to be incapable of love, which seems to find its embodiment in the curious figure of Lyduschka, to whom Balduin, characteristically, pays no attention. Balduin is prevented from loving a woman by his own personified self; and, just as his mirror-image follows him to the meetings with his beloved, so does Lyduschka follow the count's daughter like a shadow. Both these doubles intrude between the main characters in order to separate them.

Aside from these features, which the allegorical key does not explain, we are at a loss to understand what might have motivated the author, or his literary predecessors, to have represented the past in just this figure of the independently generated reflection. We also cannot comprehend, by rational thinking alone, the serious psychic results attending the loss of this image—least of all the strange death of the hero. An obscure but unavoidable feeling takes hold of the spectator and seems to betray that deep human problems are being dealt with here. The uniqueness of cinematography in visibly portraying psychological events calls our attention, with exaggerated clarity, to the fact that the interesting and meaningful problems of man's relation to himself— and the fateful disturbance of this relation—finds here an imaginative representation.

We must arrive at the meaning of these fundamental problems, necessary to understanding the film, by tracing the related forms of the motif in literary models and parallels and by comparing these forms with the corresponding folkloric, ethnographic, and mythical traditions. We should then be able to see clearly how all these motifs, originating in primitive man and his concepts, attain to literary form through those writers who are disposed to accept them. We should see also that this form coincides to a high degree with the original, and later obscured, meaning of these motifs. In the last analysis, they can be traced back to the essential problem of the ego—a problem which the modern interpreter, who is supported or compelled by the new technique of representation, has prominently highlighted by using such a vivid language of imagery.

II
Examples
of the Double
in Literature

> I imagine my ego as being
> viewed through a lens: all
> the forms which move around
> me are egos; and whatever
> they do, or leave undone,
> vexes me.
>
> E. T. A. HOFFMANN

There is not much doubt that Ewers, who has been called "the modern E. T. A. Hoffman," gained the inspiration for his film mainly from his literary predecessor and master, even though still other sources and influences were effective.[1] Hoffman is the clas-

1. Obviously, his own personal initiative—the mainspring of poetic production—cannot be in the least underrated. Those acquainted with Ewers' works do not need to be told that for a very long time he has taken special interest in the bizarre and occult phenomena of the inner life. We need only to refer to his last play *Das Wundermädchen von Berlin* (1912), which betrays isolated connections with the later screenplay *The Student of Prague*.

sical creator of the double-projection, which was among the most popular motifs in Romantic literature. Almost none of his numerous works is entirely free of references to this theme, and it predominates in many of his more significant writings. The immediate model for Ewers' treatment is in Section III ("Adventures on New Year's Eve") of the second part of the *Fantastic Tales*, entitled "The Story of the Lost Reflection" (I, 265–79).[2] In a strange connection with the imagination and dreams of the "traveling enthusiast," we read that one Erasmus Spikher, an honorable German husband and father, gets into the amorous clutches of the irresistible Giulietta during a stay in Florence and, at her request, leaves behind his reflection when he flees after murdering a rival. They were standing in front of the mirror, "which reflected him and Giulietta in a sweet embrace"; she "longingly stretched out her arms toward the mirror. Erasmus saw his image emerging independently of his movements, gliding into Giulietta's arms, and disappearing with her in a strangely sweet odor" (I, 271).

Homeward bound, Erasmus becomes an object of ridicule when people chance to notice his deficiency. Therefore, "wherever he went, he demanded that all mirrors be quickly covered, on the pretext of a natural aversion to any reflections; so people jokingly called him 'General Suvarov,' who behaved similarly" (I, 274). At home his wife spurns him and his son laughs at him. In his despair, Giulietta's mysterious companion, Doctor Dapertutto, comes to him and promises that he can regain her love and his reflection, providing that he sacrifice his wife and son to this end. The apparition of Giulietta causes him to feel love's madness anew. By taking the cloth from the mirror, she shows him how faithfully she has preserved his mirror-image. "With rapture, Erasmus saw his image folding Giulietta in its arms; but independently of himself it did not reflect any of his movements" (I, 277). He is just on the point of concluding the infernal pact, delivering himself and his family to the other-worldly powers, when he is able to exorcise the demonic spirits through the suddenly warning appearance of his wife. Then, on his wife's advice, he goes out into the wide world to seek his reflection. There he en-

2. All references to Hoffmann's works are to the 15-volume edition by Eduard Grisebach (Leipzig, 1900). A new Messter film, *Der Mann im Spiegel*, has meanwhile appeared, adapted by Robert Wiene from E. T. A. Hoffmann. [Oskar Messter, 1866–1943, was a prominent innovator in cinematography.]

counters the shadowless Peter Schlemihl, who had already appeared in the introduction to Hoffmann's story (*The Group in the Cellar*, I, 257–61). This meeting indicates that Hoffmann, in his fantastic narrative, intended to provide a counterpart to the famous "strange story" by Chamisso, the plot of which we can assume he knew.

For the sake of relevance, we will indicate briefly only the essential correspondencies and parallels. Just as with Balduin and Spikher, with Schlemihl's sale of his shadow it is also a case of bargaining with the soul (pact with the devil); and here, too, the main character receives the mockery and contempt of the world. The "gray man's" strange admiration of the shadow is especially evident as an analogy to the admiration of the mirror-image,[3] just as vanity is one of the most prominent traits of Schlemihl ("this is the spot in mankind, where the anchor catches hold most reliably"). Here too, the catastrophe—as in those cases we have already considered—is brought about through the relationship to woman. The beautiful "Fanny" is terrified by Schlemihl's lack of a shadow; and this same deficiency causes him to forfeit his life's happiness with the affectionate Mina. The insanity which became evident in Balduin as a result of his catastrophe is suggested only incidentally in Spikher and Schlemihl, both of whom are finally able to escape evil. After breaking with Mina, Schlemihl roams through "forests and plains with no goal in mind. A cold sweat dripped from my brow; a hollow groan broke from my breast; madness was raging within me."

This comparison demonstrates the equivalence of the mirror and shadow as images, both of which appear to the ego as its likeness. Later on, we shall confirm this equivalence from another point of view. Of the numerous imitations of *Peter Schlemihl* [4] we mention here only Andersen's excellent fairy tale. "The Shadow," which tells of the scholar whose shadow frees itself of its owner in the torrid zones and some years later meets him personally. At first, the loss of his shadow has no bad results at all for the man—in the manner of Schlemihl's fate—for a new shadow,

3. The "gray man" says: "During the short time that I have had the pleasure of being near you, sir, I have had the opportunity a few times—pardon me for mentioning it—of observing, really with inexpressible admiration, the beautiful shadow which you cast in the sunlight, with a certain noble disdain, as it were, without noticing the excellent shadow there at your feet."

4. Cf. Karl Goedeke, *Grundriss zur Geschichte der deutschen Dichtung* (Dresden, 1898), VI, 149 f.

though of modest proportions, appears behind him. But the first shadow, which has become very wealthy and eminent, gradually succeeds in making use of its original owner. At first, it demands of him silence concerning its earlier existence as a shadow, since it intends a betrothal. Soon, however, it carries boldness to the point of treating its former master as its shadow, thereby attracting the attention of a princess, who finally desires it as a husband. The shadow endeavors to persuade its former master, in return for a large stipend, to play the part of the shadow on all occasions. Since everything in the scholar's nature goes against this proposition, he prepares to betray this usurper of his human rights. But the shadow anticipates him and has him imprisoned. Since it assures its betrothed that its "shadow" has gone mad and believes itself to be a person, the task is easy. The night before the wedding, it effects the secret removal of the man who is dangerous to its love and thus assures itself of happiness in love.

In an intentional contrast to the story of Peter Schlemihl, this tale connects the plot of the serious results of being shadowless with the treatment of the motif as it appears in *The Student of Prague*. For in Andersen's fairy tale too, it is not simply a question of lacking something (as with Chamisso); rather, emphasis is on the pursuit by the double, which has become an independent entity and which always and everywhere balks the self—again, however, with a catastrophic effect in the relationship of love.

The loss of one's shadow, again, is more clearly emphasized in Lenau's poem "Anna," the source of which is the Swedish legend of a pretty girl who fears the loss of her beauty through childbirth.[5] *Her wish to remain always so young and beautiful* drives her, before her wedding, to a mysterious old woman who magically rids her of the seven children she would bear. She passes seven years of marriage in unchanged beauty until, one night by moonlight, her husband notices that she casts no shadow. Asked for an explanation, she confesses her guilt and becomes an outcast. After seven more years of harsh penitence and intense misery, which have left their deep traces, Anna is absolved by a her-

---

5. [See Chapter V, n. 7.] The same legend is treated by Ludwig August Frankl in his ballad "Die Kinderlose" (*Gesammelte Poetische Werke* [Vienna, 1880], II, 116), and by Hans Müller von der Leppe in his *Kronberger Liederbuch* (Frankfurt, 1895, p. 62) under the title "Fluch der Eitelkeit." Cf. also the study by J. Bolte, "Lenaus Gedicht 'Anna,'" *Euphorion*, IV (1897), 323, which provides orientation about the various versions of the legend.

mit and dies reconciled with God, after the shades of her seven
unborn children have appeared to her in a chapel.

We mention briefly the following less explicit occurrences of
the shadow-motif. Goethe's "Fairy Tale" describes a giant who
lives on the bank of a river. His shadow at noon is ineffectual and
weak but is so much the more powerful at sunrise and sunset. If
one sits down there on the neck of his shadow, one is carried
across the river simultaneously as the shadow moves. In order to
avoid this method of transportation, a bridge was built at the
spot. But when in the morning the giant rubbed his eyes, the
shadow of his fists moved so powerfully over both men and ani-
mals that all of them collapsed. Further, in Mörike's poem "The
Shadow," a count who travels to the Holy Land exacts a pledge
of loyalty from his wife. The oath is false, for his wife takes her
pleasure in the company of her lover and sends her husband a
poisoned potion that kills him. At the same hour, however, his
faithless wife also dies; only her shadow remains, inextinguish-
able, in the hall. Finally, Richard Dehmel's little poem "The
Shadow," modeled after R. L. Stevenson, describes very nicely
the puzzling character of the shadow for the child who does not
know why it has its small shadow:

> The funniest thing about him is the way he likes to grow—
> Not at all like proper children, which is always very slow;
> For he sometimes shoots up taller like an india-rubber ball,
> And he sometimes gets so little that there's none of him at all.[6]

The modes of treatment of this subject which we have so far
considered—in which the uncanny double is clearly an independent and visible cleavage of the ego (shadow, reflection)—
are different from those actual figures of the double who confront
each other as real and physical persons of unusual external similarity, and whose paths cross. Hoffmann's first novel, *The Devil's
Elixirs* (1815), depends for its effect upon a resemblance of the
monk Medardus to the Count Viktorin, both of whom are unaware that they are sons of the same father; this similarity
leads to the strangest complications. The remarkable destinies of
these two people are possible—and comprehensible—only on the
basis of this mystical presupposition. Having a pathological in-
heritance from their father, both men become mentally ill, a con-

6. [In *Robert Louis Stevenson, Collected Poems,* ed. Janet Adam Smith
(London, 1950), p. 372.] Stevenson has further treated the problem of a
double existence in his tale *The Strange Case of Doctor Jekyll and Mr.
Hyde.*

dition whose masterful description forms the chief content of the novel.[7] Viktorin, who has become insane after a fall, thinks that he is Medardus and so identifies himself to all. His identification with Medardus goes so far (poetic license, to be sure, must be taken into account) that he utters the latter's thoughts: Medardus believes that he hears himself speaking and that his innermost thoughts are being expressed by a voice outside himself.[8] This paranoiac picture is supplemented by the notions to which he is subject in the monastery, of being watched and pursued; by the erotomania associated with the picture of his beloved which he sees only momentarily; and by his morbidly intensified mistrust and self-esteem. He is also dominated by the tormenting idea of having a double who is ill, a notion confirmed by the appearance of the deranged Capuchin.

The main theme of this novel can be seen in a later development in the tale *The Doubles* (XIV, 5–52), in a clear association with rivalry for the beloved woman. Again, it is a case of two youths who are indistinguishable in external appearance and who are closely related through mysterious family circumstances. As a result of this peculiar fate, and through their love for the same girl, they get involved in the most incomprehensible adventures, the solution to which is found only when the two rivals face their beloved and voluntarily renounce all claims to her. In the *Opinions on Life of Tomcat Murr*, the same external resemblance links the fate of Kreisler, who is predisposed to mental illness, with that of the insane painter Ettlinger, whom Kreisler resembles so closely, according to Princess Hedwiga, that they could be brothers (X, 139). The situation reaches the point that Kreisler believes his reflection in the water to be the insane

7. Cf. Otto Klinke, *Hoffmanns Leben und Werke vom Standpunkt eines Irrenarztes* (2nd ed.; Braunschweig and Leipzig, 1908).

8. Dostoyevsky's novel *The Brothers Karamasov* gives a psychological insight into this aspect of the double. Before Ivan Karamasov becomes insane, the devil appears to him and acknowledges himself as his double. When Ivan comes home later one evening, a sinister gentleman enters and tells him things which Ivan himself had thought of in his youth but then forgotten. He resists acknowledging this man's reality: "Not for a minute will I accept you as a real truth. You are a lie, a disease, a phantom. I only don't know by what means I can destroy you. You are my hallucination. You are the incarnation of myself; but at that, only of one side of me . . . of my thoughts and feelings, but only of the most hideous and stupid ones. Everything . . . that has long ago been experienced, about which I long ago came to a different opinion, . . . you drag up to me, as if they were something new. You are I myself, but only in ugly caricature; you say just what I am thinking. . . ."

painter and reprimands it; but immediately thereafter he imagines that he sees his own self and his likeness walking along together (X, 146 f.). Seized by the most intense horror, he rushes
into Master Abraham's room and demands that the latter des-
patch the troublesome pursuer with a dagger (the completion of
such an impulsive act cost the student of Prague his life).

Hoffmann, who treated the problem of the second self in other
works (*Princess Brambilla, The Heart of Stone, The Choice of a
Bride, The Sandman,* and others), doubtless had strong personal
motives for this choice of theme; yet one cannot underestimate
the influence exercised by Jean Paul, who introduced the motif
of the double into Romantic literature and who at this time was
at the height of his fame.[9] In Jean Paul's works this theme predominates in all its psychological variants. Leibgeber and Siebenkäs are real doubles: they look exactly alike, and Siebenkäs
even exchanges names with his friend. In *Siebenkäs* the constant
confusion between these persons—a motif elsewhere frequent
with Jean Paul (e.g., in *Katzenberger's Trip to the Spa*)—is the
central point of interest; in *Titan* it occurs only episodically. In
addition to this occurrence of the double as an actual person—
which Jean Paul also varies by having someone attempt to seduce
the beloved in the shape of the lover (the Amphytrion-motif)—
this writer has delineated again and again, and to an extreme, the
problem of the splitting and reduplication of the ego as no one
has done before or after him.

"In *Hesperus* he causes his ego to arise before him as an uncanny apparition" (Schneider, p. 317). In his childhood, Viktor is
particularly aroused by those stories in which people see themselves. "Often, before going to sleep at night, he observes his
body so long that he separates it from himself and sees it standing
and gesticulating next to himself. Then he goes to sleep with this
strange figure" (Czerny, p. 11). Viktor also had a violent aversion
to wax figures, a feeling which he has in common with Ottomar
(*The Invisible Lodge*), who in a trance sees his ego in the air.
This horror of figures made of wax becomes understandable in
Titan, when Albano crushes his own wax bust in helpless rage;
but in doing so he feels "that he is touching, and murdering, his
Self" (Schneider, p. 318). Schoppe and Albano are possessed by

9. Cf. here and following F. J. Schneider, *Jean Pauls Jugend und sein
Auftreten in der Literatur* (Berlin, 1905), esp. pp. 316–320; cf. also Jo-
hann Czerny, "Jean Pauls Beziehungen zu E. T. A. Hoffmann," *Gymn.
Progr. Mies* (1906–1907 and 1907–1908, pp. 5–23).

the destructive delusion of a double who is pursuing them. Albano's mirrored self, which has been running along beside him, frightens him away from the dream-temple into which he has wandered. "Leibgeber in *Siebenkäs,* too, sees himself surrounded by an army of Selves in comparing his ego, his and Firmian's, the reflection of his double—three egos—with Firmian himself, the fourth. . . . Firmian steps to the mirror and with a finger presses his eyeball sideways so that he sees two reflections of himself; he then turns pityingly to his friend with the words, 'But you really can't see the third person there'" (Schneider, p. 318).

In *Titan* we again come across the tendency toward depersonalization, which is indicated by the name 'Leibgeber.' Roquairol, who is described as a boundless egoist, once does long to have a friend and writes to Albano: "Then I saw you, and wanted to become your You—but that won't work, for I cannot go back; but you can go on ahead, one of these days you will become my Self" (Schneider, p. 32).[10] "Performing his own tragedy, mimicking his own ego, he kills himself" (Schneider, p. 320). "Schoppe's notion of being chased by himself becomes a most dreadful torment. For him, blissfulness lies in being eternally rid of his ego. If his glance only by chance falls upon his hands or his legs, that is enough to cause the cold fear to come over him that he could appear to himself and see his ego. The mirror must be veiled, for he shakes with fright before the spectacle of his mirror-orangutan" (Schneider, p. 318).

There are also mirrors which cause rejuvenation and aging, a motif which seems to have been transferred to Spikher, whose old and distorted face grins at him on one occasion (similarly, there are pictures whose proper lines can be recognized only under one particular lens). We recall here that Spikher too, like Balduin, has all mirrors covered: "but for the contrary reason, that they no

10. Richard Dehmel, the paraphraser of the shadow-poem by Stevenson, has expressed the same tendency in the beautiful poem "Masks," which describes how the poet at a masked ball vainly seeks himself in various masks and concludes each stanza with the words, "You are not I—but I am you." Finally, he finds that which he seeks:

And you—it's you—you *mirror'd* domino,
Wherein the hues, like ocean's tints, do reel,
You face without a mask: the seal me show,
That, of your thoughts, the sources will reveal:
Is't you yourself? A sign—you nod to me:
Archaic seal and mask—do *me* I see?

longer may reflect his ego" (Czerny, p. 12). With Schoppe, this fear goes so far that he even smashes the hated mirrors, since they cause his Self to move toward him. And just as Kreisler and Balduin want to slay their second selves, Schoppe sends his sword-cane to Albano with the demand that the latter do away with the uncanny apparition in Ratto's cellar. "Schoppe finally perishes of his delusion, with the declaration of his identity on his lips" (Schneider, p. 319).

It is known that Jean Paul in *Titan* expressed his views on Fichte's philosophy and intended to show what would be the ultimate consequence of transcendental idealism. Critics have argued whether the poet merely meant to present his opinions to the philosopher or to lead him *ad absurdum*. However that may be, it seems clear in any case that both tried, each in his own way, to arrive at an understanding of the problem of the ego —a problem which concerned them personally.

From the corporeal figures of the double, we can pass, by way of some individual and original treatments, over to those representations which allow us to recognize the subjective limitation and meaning of the strange attitude. One of them is Ferdinand Raimund's Romantic-comic fable *The King of the Alps and the Misanthropist*, in which the double of the wealthy Rappelkopf is represented by the Spirit of the Alps, objectified with genuine Raimund naïveté. Rappelkopf, who appears disguised as his brother-in-law, sees a performance of his own ridiculous faults and weaknesses by Astralagus, the King of the Alps, who plays the part of Rappelkopf himself. The action brings about the cure of the hero of his hypochondriacal misanthropy and his paranoiac mistrust by having him look at his own self as if in a "mirror of the soul." Through this sight he learns to hate himself and to love the surroundings which he earlier hated so much.

It is noteworthy that some typical motifs of the double-phenomenon seem here to be raised from their unconscious tragedy into the cognitive sphere of humor. In the end, the stubborn Rappelkopf agrees to the exchange of souls as if to a joke; and the confrontation of the two doubles in the main scenes of the play leads to multiple confusions and complications. The hero finally does not know where to look for his self and remarks, "I am afraid of myself." These "damned carryings-on with doubles" finally lead to mutual insults and to duelling.

The impulse to rid oneself of the uncanny opponent in a violent manner belongs, as we saw, to the essential features of the motif; and when one yields to this impulse—as, for example, in *The Student of Prague* and in other treatments which we still have to discuss—it becomes clear that the life of the double is linked quite closely to that of the individual himself. In Raimund's play, this mysterious basis of the problem becomes a conscious requisite of the test. In the last moment before the duel, Rappelkopf recalls this condition: "Both of us have only one life. If I kill him, I will kill myself." He is released from the spell when Astralagus plunges into the water: Rappelkopf, who fears drowning, falls into a swoon and awakes cured. Especially interesting to us is a remnant of the mirror-motif, pointing to the inner significance of the double. At the height of his delusion shortly before his flight from home and family, Rappelkopf catches sight of himself in the tall pier glass in his room. He is unable to endure the sight of his face and "shatters the mirror with his clenched fist." But in a tall pier glass in Rappelkopf's house, the King of the Alps then becomes visible and later appears as a double.

Raimund has treated the same theme in a different form in *The Spendthrift*. The beggar, who for a year has been following Flottwell everywhere, turns out twenty years later to be his double and saves him from total ruin—in the way of a protective spirit, as is the King of the Alps. Flottwell actually believes that this beggar is the spirit of his father, until, taught by his harsh fate, he recognizes in the warning figure himself at the age of fifty. Here, too, the pursued attempts to kill his burdensome companion but is unable to attack in any way. The relationship of this double to that which appears in *The King of the Alps* is indicated by a common motif, the psychological discussion of which is more relevant elsewhere. Just as the beggar wheedles treasures from Flottwell in order to return them to the completely impoverished man ("I have begged from you for you"), so Rappelkopf, who likewise is apparently poor and in the end becomes rich again, gives a comic turn to this motif of the "jointly-held funds" by picking up the money cast aside by his double with the remark that this joint ownership is a far more convenient arrangement than the undesirable mutual ownership of health and life.

Even though there is an interesting connection here between the theme of aging and the financial complex which is not taken into account here, this or that thread of reference to the problem of the double can be traced. The fact that the beggar appears in the shape of Flottwell twenty years older reminds us of the girl's belief that looking at the King of the Alps makes one forty years older. And when the King appears in the mirror, Lieschen shuts her eyes so that she might not lose her beauty. In this we can note the connection with Jean Paul's mirrors, which can make one old or young, as well as with the distorting mirrors in Hoffmann's works and those of other writers.

This fear of becoming old, as one of the deepest problems of the self, is treated in Oscar Wilde's novel *The Picture of Dorian Gray* (1890 [1891]). The handsome and vigorous Dorian, when viewing his well-done portrait, expresses the presumptuous desire always to remain so young and handsome and to be able to transfer any traces of age and of sin to the portrait—a wish to be fulfilled in a sinister way. He first notices a change in the picture when Sibyl, who loves him above all else, cruelly and coldly repulses him (just as most of his similarly destined parallels become deranged in love for woman). From then on the portrait, constantly aging and betraying the marks of sin, continues to be the visible conscience of Dorian. It teaches him, who loves himself inordinately, to despise his own soul. He covers and locks up the picture which inspires him with fear and terror, only gazing at it in particular moments of his life and comparing it with his own eternally immutable mirror-image. His former delight in his handsomeness gradually gives way to an abhorrence of his own self. Finally, ". . . he loathed his own beauty, and, flinging the mirror on the floor, crushed it into silver splinters beneath his heel." A definitely neurotic spectrophobia, related with great artistic effect, is the theme of one of Dorian's favorite novels, whose main character, quite in contrast to Dorian, had lost his extraordinary beauty in his early youth. Since then, he had a ". . . grotesque dread of mirrors, and polished metal surfaces, and still water. . . ."

After Dorian has murdered the painter of the fateful picture and has driven Sibyl to death, he no longer finds any rest: "The consciousness of being hunted, snared, tracked down, had begun to dominate him." He decides to bring matters to a close and to destroy the picture, in this way freeing himself from his unendurable past. He stabs the picture and, in the same moment, old and ugly falls dead with the knife in his heart, while the picture shows him in his unstained youthful handsomeness.[11]

11. [Oscar Wilde, *The Picture of Dorian Gray* (Cleveland and New York, 1946), pp. 249, 149, 227. Further references will be to this edition.] Claude Farrère has skillfully treated the motif of sudden aging in *Das*

Of other Romanticists who dealt with the double-motif—and in one form or another it was used by almost all of them[12]— Heine may be mentioned briefly. The double, which in the opinion of scholarship is one of his basic motifs, likewise appears not as a corporeal counterpart, but rather in a more subjective form.[13] "In *Ratcliff* he intends to describe the fate of two persons whose lives are filled with meaninglessness through being compelled to exist as doubles—persons who must murder each other although they are in love. Their daily existence is constantly criss-crossed by their ancestral lives, which they are forced to live once again. This compulsion brings about the split in their personalities." [Rank does not give the source of this quotation.] Ratcliff obeys an inner voice which admonishes him to murder anyone who approaches Marie.

The motif is found in a different form in *Nights in Florence,* as exemplified by the double existence of Madame Laurencer. Her cheerful life in the daytime alternates with terpsichorean ecstasies at night, and she speaks of them by day calmly as of something long past. A similar narrative is in *Atta Troll* about the dead Laskaro, "whose loving mother every night rubs a magic life into him with the [a?] most powerful ointment." In *Germany, a Winter's Tale* (Ch. VI), a queer fellow always appears to the poet when he is sitting at his desk at night. Upon being questioned, this person acknowledges: "I am the action of your thoughts." There are also similar references in several of Heine's poems. [*Deutschland, Ein Wintermärchen,* Ch. VII. *Junge Leiden:* "Im nächtgen Traum hab' ich mich selbst geschaut"; "Im Traum sah ich ein Männchen klein und putzig"; *Die Heimkehr:* "Still ist die Nacht, es ruhen die Gassen"; "Gaben mir Rat und gute Lehren."]

One can see that these treatments of the motif come close to an extreme which has only a somewhat loose connection with our topic. Up to this point, it has been a question either of a

Geheimnis der Lebenden (Frankfurt, 1912). It appears in a superficial form in Leo Perutz and Paul Frank, *Das Mangobaumwunder* (Munich, n.d. [1916]).

12. In Tieck, Arnim, and Brentano the double-motif is used primarily in the external form of confused identities or in the solution of complicated plots by the identification of various persons; in Novalis and others it is used in a mystic vagueness; in Fouqué (*Der Zauberring,* II, 13), Kerner (*Die Reiseschatten*), and others it is used only episodically.

13. Helene Herrmann, *Studien zu Heines Romanzero* (Berlin, 1906). Cf. also W. Siebert, "Heines Beziehungen zu Hoffmann," in *Beiträge zur deutschen Literaturwissenschaft* (Marburg, 1908), Vol. VII.

physical double, which takes a more distantly related form in the comedies of mistaken identities) [14] or of a likeness which has been detached from the ego and become an individual being (shadow, reflection, portrait). Now we come upon the representationally opposite form of expression of the same psychic constellation: the representation, by one and the same person, of two distinct beings separated by amnesia. These cases of double-consciousness have also been observed clinically[15] and have been presented quite often in recent literary works,[16] though they need not be an object of our further investigation.[17]

From these marginal cases, we turn again to those subjects more fruitful for our analysis. In them the figure of a double is more or less clearly shaped but, at the same time, appears as the spontaneous subjective creation of a morbidly active imagination. Those cases of double-consciousness which we do not consider here—but which appear psychologically as the basis, and representationally as a kind of preliminary stage, of the fully-developed double-delusion—include Maupassant's impressive tale *The Horla* (1887), which serves as a direct transition over to the classification which is of interest to us.

The main character, whose diary we read, suffers from anxiety-reactions that torment him especially at night, pursue him even in his dreams, and cannot be permanently dispelled by any remedy. One night, he discovers to his terror that his carafe, filled at evening, is completely empty, although no one could

---

14. Mistaken identity, the immortal subject of comedy, was certain of its effect from Plautus' *Menaechmi* down to Ludwig Fulda's *Die Zwillings-schwester* (Frankfurt, 1901). Well-known examples are Shakespeare, *Comedy of Errors;* Lecoque, *Giroflé-Giroflá;* and Nestroy, *Der Färber und sein Zwillingsbruder.*

15. Cf. the informative work by Max Dessoir, *Das Doppel-Ich* (2nd ed.; Leipzig, 1896).

16. See, for example, the famous novel by George du Maurier, *Trilby,* later made into a play; Hugh Conway, "Called Back"; Dick-May, "L'affaire Allard" (in *Unheimliche Geschichten*); Paul Lindau's drama *Der Andere,* lately also made into a film; and Georg Hirschfeld, "Das zweite Leben."

17. We disregard entirely the occult concept of the double-phenomenon, since it is interpreted as the simultaneous existence of the same individual at two different places. As a typical example of this treatment, cf. August Strindberg, "Inferno. Legenden," translated into German by Emil Schering, [*Strindbergs Dramaturgie* (Munich, 1911)], Vol. IV, Part 4, pp. 50 ff., 285 ff., etc. In many writings of Strindberg, the split of the personality is carried to the extreme (cf. especially the novel *Am offenen Meere*). On Strindberg's paranoia, cf. the pathography by S. Rahmer in *Grenzfragen der Literatur und Medizin* (1907), fasc. 6.

enter the locked room. From this moment on, his entire interest concentrates upon that invisible spirit—the Horla—who lives in him, or next to him. He makes attempts to escape it in every way, but in vain; he is only more and more convinced of the independent existence of the mysterious creature. Everywhere he feels that it overhears him, watches him, enters into his thoughts, controls him, pursues him. Often he turns around in a split second, to see it at last, and to grasp it. Often he rushes into the empty darkness of his room, where he thinks the Horla is, in order "to seize it, to throttle it, to kill it."

Finally, this thought of being rid of the invisible tyrant gains the upper hand: he has the windows and doors of his room fitted with iron shutters which can be firmly locked, and he cautiously steals out one evening to imprison the Horla inescapably behind him. Then he sets the house on fire and, from a distance, watches as it is destroyed together with any living creatures inside. But, in the end, he is beset by doubts whether the Horla, for which all this was intended, could actually be destroyed; and he sees no other way to escape from it except by killing himself.[18] Here again, the death which is intended for the ego as a double strikes down instead the person himself. How far his disintegration goes here is shown by a mirror-fantasy which occurs prior to the decisive catastrophe. The hero has brightly illuminated his room in order to lie in wait for the Horla:

Behind me stands a tall wardrobe with a mirror, which daily assisted me in shaving and getting dressed and in which I looked at myself from head to toe every time I walked past it. I was pretending to write, to deceive him, for he was watching for me also. And suddenly I felt—I knew very well what I was doing—that he was bending over my shoulder and reading, that he was there, and that he brushed against my ear. I stood up, stretched out my hands, and turned around so quickly that I almost fell. What now? One could see as well here as if the sun were shining, and *I did not see myself in my mirror.* The glass was empty, clear, deep, brightly lit, but my reflection was missing, though I was standing where it would be cast. I looked at the large, clear, mirrored surface from top to bottom, looked at it with horrified eyes! I no longer dared to step forward; I dared make no movement; I felt that he was there but that again he would escape me, he whose opaque body prevented my reflecting myself. And— how terrible!—suddenly I saw myself in a mist in the center of the mirror, through a sort of watery veil; and it seemed to me as if this

18. In a similar portrayal by J. E. Poritzky [*Gespenstergeschichten* (2nd ed.; Munich, 1913)], "the unknown" is Death, which likewise incessantly and invisibly follows the character.

water were slipping from left to right, very slowly, so that my image appeared more sharply outlined from second to second. . . . Finally I could recognize myself as fully as I do every day when glancing into the mirror. I had seen him; and even now I am still trembling with fright.

In a small sketch, *He,* which gives the impression of being a draft for *The Horla,* Maupassant has caused some features of interest to us to emerge more prominently—for example, a man's relationship to a woman. The entire narrative about the mysterious "he"—who inspires the main character with a dreadful fear of himself—appears as the confession of a man who wants to marry, must marry, against his better judgment, simply because he can no longer endure being alone at night after once, upon coming home, having seen "him" occupying his own accustomed place in the armchair by the fireplace.[19] "He pursues me incessantly. That's madness! Yet it is so. Who, he? I know very well that he does not exist, that he is unreal. He lives only in my misgivings, in my fears, in my anxiety!—But when I am living with someone, I feel clearly, yes, quite clearly, he will no longer exist. For he exists only because I am alone, solely because I am alone!"

This same atmosphere has found moving expression, shaded with melancholy resignation, in Musset's "December Night" (1835). In a dialogue with the "vision," the poet tells us that since his childhood a shadowy double who resembles him like a brother has been following him always and everywhere. In the decisive moments of his life this companion appears, clothed in black. He cannot escape this companion however far he flees, and he is unable to ascertain its nature. And just as once upon a time, as a youth in love, he found himself alone with his double,[20] so now, many years later, he is absorbed one night in sweet memories of that time of love, and the apparition reveals itself again. The poet seeks to fathom its essence. He addresses it as his evil

19. The theme is treated similarly in Kipling's ["At the End of the Passage," in *Life's Handicap,* London, 1892, p. 261]: Hummil sees himself sitting at the table when he comes there, and the apparition hurries away: "Except that it cast no shadow it was in all respects real."

20. The stanza reads:

When youthful love my mind beguiled,
One day lorn in my room I wiled,
My first affliction to deplore.
Near my hearth came to a chair
An alien one, who black did wear,
And a brother's semblance bore.

fate, as his good angel, and finally, when he cannot banish love's memories, as his own reflection:

> But all at once I saw, in th' nocturnal gloom,
>   A noiseless form glide apace.
> I saw a shadow o'er my curtain loom,
>   Upon my bed it took its place.
> Who art thou, countenance so pale and drear,
>   Somber likeness of sable hue?
> Sad fleeting bird, why just to me appear?
> Is it an empty dream, *my* image here,
>   Which within this mirror comes to view?

In the end, the apparition identifies itself as "Solitude." Even though it may seem strange at first glance that solitude, as with Maupassant, is perceived and represented as the burdensome companionship of a second being, the emphasis lies—as Nietzsche, too, stated—on the sociability with one's own self, objectified as a duplication. A similar monologue with one's own personified self is the foundation of Jean Paul's *The Devil's Confession to an Eminent Official.*[21] The same motif takes an interesting psychological turn in the story by J. E. Poritzky entitled *One Night.*[22] One evening, "a Doctor Faust in age and wisdom" apparently joins the main character of this fine little sketch for a

---

21. There are similar occurrences in Coleridge (*Poems*) and in Baudelaire (*Les Fleurs du Mal*). Of the former, the poem ["Phantom or Fact? A Dialogue in Verse"] may be mentioned which, like Musset's verses, gives a dialogue between a friend and the poet, to whom his own true self appears:

> Call it a moment's work (and such it seems)
> This tale's a fragment from the life of dreams;
> But say, that years matur'd the silent strife,
> And 'tis a record from the dream of life.

[See *The Complete Works of Samuel Taylor Coleridge*, ed. Professor Shedd (New York, 1853), VII, 280.]

We may give here as an example from Baudelaire a stanza from "The Gaming Table":

> My eye, turned inward, darkly can discern
> This Hellish picture self-distorted thus,
> The while I see in yonder taciturn
> Corner myself, cold, mute—and envious.

[See Charles Baudelaire, *The Flowers of Evil*, translated by Humbert Wolfe and edited by Marthiel and Jackson Mathews (Norfolk, Conn., 1963), pp. 121–122.]

Frank Wedekind, in his poem "Der Gefangene," has described the impossibility of escaping the concept of one's own self.

22. Poritzky, *op. cit.* In the tale "Im Reiche der Geister" in this volume, his double appears mysteriously to the student Orest Najaddin (p. 84).

serious conversation, abundant in recollections. The previous night, so the old man relates, he had the experience at midnight of being seized in front of his mirror by a childhood memory that contained the superstitious fear of gazing into a mirror at midnight. "I smiled upon remembering this and stepped before the mirror, as though intending to give the lie to the legends of youth and to scorn them. I glanced into it, but since my mind was completely filled with thoughts of my boyhood years and I inwardly viewed myself as I had appeared as a boy—I had completely forgotten, as it were, my present existence—I stared fixedly and with distaste into the wrinkled old man's face which gazed at me from the mirror." This bizarre state of mind reaches the point that the figure before the mirror shouts for help in his former boyish tones. The old man wants to protect the vision which has suddenly disappeared. He tries to justify the experience:

I am very well aware of the division in our consciousness. Everyone has felt it more or less intensely—that division in which one sees one's own person passing by, like a shadow, in all of the shapes in which he ever existed. . . .[23] But it is also possible for us now and then to catch sight of our future modes of existence. . . . This view of our future self is sometimes so vivid that we think that we see alien persons as independent entities physically detaching themselves from us, as a child at birth. And then, one meets these apparitions of the future, conjured up from one's self, and greets them with a nod. That is my secret discovery.[24] We are indebted to the French psychologist Ribot for some very odd examples of psychic cleavage which cannot be explained away simply as hallucinations. A very intelligent man possessed the ability of conjuring up his double before him. He would always laugh loudly at this vision, and his double responded with the same laughter. This dangerous entertainment amused him for a long time, but it finally came to a bad end. He gradually arrived at the conviction that he *was being pursued by himself*; and since his second self constantly tormented, teased, and annoyed him, he decided one day to put an end to this sad existence.

After citing an additional example, the old man asks his companion whether he had never felt old, despite his thirty-five

23. As in Musset's verses.
24. Cf. here the dream of Friedrich Hebbel's wife, communicated in his diaries (June 3, 1847), in which she sees in a mirror her entire future life. First, she sees her quite youthful face becoming older and older, and finally she turns away in the fear that her skeleton will now appear. Cf. also Hebbel's entry of December 15, 1846: "Someone who sees himself in the mirror and cries for help, because he thinks he sees a stranger; this 'stranger' has been put there with paint."

years. Upon receiving a negative answer, the old man takes his leave. His companion seeks to shake hands, but to his astonishment only air meets his grasp; he sees no one either near or far. "I was alone, and opposite me was a mirror which held me captive. Only now, when it had released my eyes, did I see that the candle had burned down low. . . . Had I spoken with myself? Had I departed from my body and returned to it only now? Who knows . . . ? Or *had I confronted myself, like Narcissus,* and then had encountered the future shapes of my own self, and greeted them? Who knows . . . ?"

In his short story *William Wilson,* Edgar Allan Poe used the theme of the double in a way that has become a model for several later treatments. William Wilson, the main character of this first-person narrative, meets a double in his childhood at school. The double not only has Wilson's own name and birthday, but also resembles him so much in physique, speech, behavior, and gait that both of them are considered to be brothers—indeed, even twins. Soon this strange namesake, who imitates Wilson in everything, becomes his faithful comrade, inseparable companion, and finally his most feared rival. Only by his voice, which cannot rise above a whisper, is the double distinguishable from his original; but this voice is identical in accent and pronunciation, so that ". . . *his singular whisper, it grew the very echo of my own.*"[25]

Despite this uncanny imitation, the main character is incapable of hating his counterpart; nor is he able to reject the "advice not openly given, but hinted or insinuated" [original text] which he obeys, but only with repugnance. This tolerance is justified to some extent by the fact that the counterpart is apparently perceived only by the main character himself and attracts no further [sic] attention from his companions. One circumstance—the mention of his name—irritated Wilson without exception: "The words were venom in my ears; and when, upon the day of my arrival, a second William Wilson came also to the academy, I felt angry with him for bearing the name and doubly disgusted with the name because a stranger bore it, who would be the cause of its twofold repetition. . . ." One night the hero sneaks into his double's bedroom in order to convince himself that the features of the sleeper cannot be the result of a mere sarcastic imitation.

25. Cf. also E. A. Poe, *Shadow. A Parable.* [Quotations from *William Wilson* are taken from the text in *Burton's Gentleman's Magazine and American Monthly Review,* V (1839), 205–212.]

He flees in terror from the school and, after some months at home, goes to study at Eton, where he begins to lead a life of profligacy. He has long since forgotten the uncanny episode at the academy, but one night at a carousal his double appears to him in the same modish attire as his own, but with indistinct facial features. With only the warningly whispered words "William Wilson," the double disappears. All attempts to discover this person's identity and whereabouts are useless, except for the information that he had disappeared from the academy on the same day as his prototype.

Soon Wilson goes to Oxford, where he continues his extremely luxurious life and morally sinks lower and lower—not even shrinking from the stratagems of cheating at cards. One night when he has just won large sums in this way at a game, his double suddenly enters and reveals his tricks. In confusion and disgrace, Wilson is compelled the next morning to leave both the room and Oxford. Like Musset's poet, he flees restlessly from place to place through all of Europe, but everywhere the double interferes with his undertakings, always, to be sure, in ways designed to prevent mischief.

The catastrophe finally comes at a masked ball in Rome after Wilson has determined to rid himself, at any cost, of the unknown's oppressive tyranny. At just the moment when Wilson is trying to approach the charming wife of his aging host, a hand grasps him by the shoulder. He recognizes his double by the identical costume, drags him into an adjoining room, and challenges him to a duel. After a brief passage at arms, he plunges his sword into the double's heart. Someone tries the latch of the door and Wilson turns away momentarily. Suddenly, however, the situation surprisingly changes:

A large mirror—so at first it seemed to me in my confusion—now stood where none had been perceptible before; and as I stepped up to it in extremity of terror, mine own image, but with features all pale and dabbled in blood, advanced to meet me with a feeble and tottering gait. Thus it appeared, I say, but was not. It was my antagonist—it was Wilson who then stood before me in the agonies of his dissolution. His mask and cloak lay where he had thrown them upon the floor. Not a thread in all his raiment—not a line in all the marked and singular lineaments of his face—which was not, even in the most absolute identity, *mine own!* It was Wilson; but he spoke no longer in a whisper, and I could have fancied that I myself was speaking while he said: *"You have conquered, and I yield. Yet henceforward art thou also dead—dead to the World, to Heaven, and to*

Hope! In me didst thou exist; and in my death see by this image, which is thine own, how utterly thou hast murdered thyself!"

The most moving, and psychologically the most profound, treatment of our theme is probably Dostoyevsky's early novel *The Double* (1846). The novel describes the onset of mental illness in a person who is not aware of it, since he is unable to recognize the symptoms in himself, and who paranoiacally views all his painful experiences as the pursuits of his enemies. His gradual transition into a delusional state, and confusion with reality (the real theme of this work otherwise sparse in external events) is depicted with an unsurpassable skill. We recognize the great artistic accomplishment here by the completely objective descriptions; they include not only every feature of the paranoiac clinical picture, but also cause the delusional configurations to have an effect upon the environment of the victim himself. The development of the story until its catastrophe is compressed into a few days and can hardly be reproduced except through reprinting the entire tale. We can only recapitulate here, though briefly, the essential points.

The unfortunate hero of the story, Titularrat Golyadkin, dresses himself one morning with particular care and elegance. Instead of going to his office, he intends to drive to a dinner at the house of Counselor Berendeyeff, his "benefactor since time immemorial who, in a certain sense, has taken the place of my father." On the way there, however, all sorts of events occur which cause him to alter his purpose. From his carriage, he notices two young co-workers from the office, one of whom appears to point to him while the other loudly calls his name. Irritated by "these stupid youths," he is upset by a new and even more painful experience: past his carriage rolls the elegant coach of the head of his department, Andrei Filippovich, who is obviously surprised to see his subordinate under such circumstances. "In an indescribably tormenting anxiety," Golyadkin asks himself, "Shall I recognize him, or should I act as if I were not myself at all, but rather some other person who is confusingly similar to me?" "Yes, to be sure, I am simply not myself . . . quite simply, I am a completely different person, and no one else." And he does not greet his superior.

As he ruefully reflects upon this bit of foolishness and the malice of his enemies which forced him to commit it, Mr. Golyadkin feels "the compelling need, for his own peace of mind, to

tell something very important to his physician Krestjan Ivanovich," although he has known him only for a few days. He con-
fides to the doctor in detail, with the most acute embarrassment
and the characteristic vagueness of paranoids, that enemies are
pursuing him—"detestable enemies who have plotted to destroy me." He mentions, incidentally, that they would not shrink
from using poison but that they primarily intend his moral death,
in which regard his mysteriously hinted relationship with a
woman is the main concern. This person, a German cook with
whom he is being mentioned in a slanderous connection, and
Klara Olssufyevna, the daughter of his old patron whom he intended to visit at the beginning of the story, dominate his extremely subtle and characteristically presented erotomanic fantasies. In the conviction that "the entire power of the evil forces
is concealed in the nest of these detestable Germans," he shame-
fully confesses to the doctor that both the head of the department and his nephew, who has just been promoted and is wooing
Klara, have been spreading rumors about Golyadkin. He says
that he had to give the cook, in whose home he formerly
dwelled, a written promise of marriage instead of payment for
his meals; that he is therefore "already the fiancé of someone
else."

At the home of the Councillor, where he appears a little
ahead of time, he is told that he will not be admitted. Embarrassed, he has to depart, and he sees the other guests enter,
among them the department head and his nephew. Later, and
under embarrassing circumstances, he does intrude upon the
celebration held in honor of Klara's birthday. On the occasion of
congratulations upon this event, his extremely awkward behavior offends everyone. Then, when he stumbles while dancing
with Klara, he is forcibly ejected from the place.

At midnight, "in order to be rescued from his enemies," he
rushes aimlessly through the deserted streets of St. Petersburg
during a terrible storm. He looks "as if he wanted to hide from
himself, as if he wanted, most of all, to run away from himself."
Exhausted and in nameless despair, he finally comes to a stop beside the canal and leans on its railing. Suddenly "it seemed to
him that at that moment someone had been standing closely beside him, likewise leaning on the railing, and—strange!—it
was as if this person had even said something to him, quickly and
briefly and not quite clearly, but something that closely concerned him, that had a personal meaning to him."

After this strange apparition Golyadkin tries to regain his composure; but as he walks on, he is approached by a man whom he takes to be the leader of the intrigue directed against him. As the man comes closer, he terrifies Golyadkin through a strikingly similar appearance: "He too was walking very hastily, was likewise all muffled up . . . and, like Mr. Golyadkin, walked with small, quick, tripping steps. . . ." To his boundless astonishment, the same unknown man encounters him yet a third time. Golyadkin runs after him, calls to him, but sees by the gleam of the nearest street-lamp that his impression was mistaken. In spite of this, he does not doubt that he knows the man very well: "He even knew the fellow's surname, nickname, and patronymic. But yet, even for all the world's treasures, he would not have called him by name."

While reflecting further on the matter, he begins to desire the mysterious encounter which now seems unavoidable, the sooner the better. In fact, soon thereafter the unknown man walks along a short distance in front of him. At this time our hero is on his way home, which the unmistakable double appears to know exactly. He enters Mr. Golyadkin's house, nimbly hastens up the hazardous stairs, and at last enters the apartment, the servant having promptly opened the door. When Mr. Golyadkin breathlessly enters his room, "the unknown man was sitting before him on his bed, likewise with his hat and coat on." Incapable of giving vent to his feelings, Golyadkin "sat down rigid with terror next to the other one. . . . Mr. Golyadkin immediately recognized his nocturnal friend. But this nocturnal friend was none other than he himself—yes, Mr. Golyadkin himself, another Mr. Golyadkin and yet Mr. Golyadkin himself; in a word, and in every respect, he was what is termed a double."

The powerful impression of this experience at the end of the day is reflected the next morning by an increase in ideas of persecution. These ideas now appear more and more clearly to emanate from the double, who soon takes on a physical form and no longer disappears from the center of the delusional images. At the office, where he must expect to receive "a rebuke for neglect of duty," the hero finds a new employee on the seat next to his—none other than the second Mr. Golyadkin. He is "a different Mr. Golyadkin, completely different, and yet at the same time one who perfectly resembled the first—of the same stature, of the same physique and bearing, in the same clothes, likewise bald; in brief, nothing, nothing whatever had been overlooked in this complete similarity. If the two of them had been placed next to each other, no one, absolutely no one, would have been able to say who was the real Mr. Golyadkin and who the imitation, who the old and who the new, who the original and who the copy." But yet this exact "reflection," who even bears the same given names and comes from the same town, is the antithesis to his prototype in traits of character. Although the two are considered to be twins, the double is venturesome, hypocritical, sycophantic, and ambitious. Knowing how to attain popularity with everyone, he soon eliminates his clumsy, timid, pathologically candid rival.[26]

The relationship of Mr. Golyadkin to his double which now develops, and the description of which forms the main content of the novel, can receive our attention here only in its most significant aspects. At first, an extremely intimate friendship comes about. There is even an alliance against the foes of the hero, who tells his new friend the most important secrets: "I love, love you, love you like a brother, I tell you. But together, Sasha, we shall play a trick on them." Soon, however, Golyadkin suspects that his image is his chief enemy and tries to protect himself against this threat, both at the office, where his double brings him into disfavor with his co-workers and superiors, as well as in his personal affairs, in which the double seems to be winning Klara's affections.

The offensive fellow even pursues the hero in his dreams, in which, fleeing from his double, he sees himself surrounded by a large crowd of self-replicas from whom he cannot escape.[27] But even in his waking hours this uncanny relationship torments him to the point that he finally challenges his opponent to a duel with pistols. Here too, besides this typical motif, the mirror-scenes are not lacking, the significance of which seems to be enhanced by the fact that the narrative begins with one of them. "He had scarcely jumped out of bed, when the first thing he did was to rush to the round little mirror which stood on his dresser. And although the sleepy face, with its myopic eyes and rather sparse hair above, which gazed out at him from the mirror was

26. Traces of his career here and there are strikingly reminiscent of the main theme of E. T. A. Hoffmann's fairy tale "Klein Zaches" [genannt Zinnober].

27. A similar anxiety-dream of numerous images of one's own self is found in Jerome K. Jerome, Studies in the Novel [not by this author, nor has a search disclosed which work Rank had in mind here].

so ordinary that it quite definitely could not have arrested the attention of any other person, its owner nevertheless appeared to be very well satisfied with what he was experiencing."

At the point of the most tireless pursuit by his double—when Golyadkin takes a small pie at the buffet of a restaurant—he is charged ten times its price, with explicit reference to his having eaten so much. His speechless astonishment yields to comprehension when he glances up and recognizes the other Mr. Golyadkin in the door opposite him, "which our hero had previously considered to be a mirror." He has been mistaken for his double, who has presumed to expose him in this way. The hero becomes the victim of a similar deception when, in the greatest despair, he goes to see his highest-ranking chief in order to entrust himself to his "fatherly protection." The awkward conversation with His Excellency is suddenly interrupted by "a peculiar guest. In the door, which until now our hero had taken to be a mirror, as had already happened to him once, he appeared; we already know who: Mr. Golyadkin's acquaintance and friend."

Through his strange behavior toward his co-workers and superiors, Golyadkin manages to get himself dismissed from his position. But the real catastrophe, like that of all other main characters who have doubles, bears a reference to a woman, to Klara Olssufyevna. Involved in correspondence with his double and with Vachrameyeff, one of the "defenders" of the "German cook," Golyadkin receives a letter secretly delivered which rekindles his erotomanic fantasies. In this letter Klara Olssufyevna asks him to protect her from a marriage forced on her against her will. She wants him to run away with her, who has already fallen prey to a scoundrel's guile and who now entrusts herself to her noble rescuer. After much thought and reflection the mistrustful Golyadkin decides to assent to this appeal and to be in a carriage in front of Klara's house at nine in the evening, as she requested.

On the way to this rendezvous, however, he undertakes one last attempt to set things in order. As before a father, he wants to cast himself at His Excellency's feet and implore rescue from his vile double. He will say: "He is a different person, Your Excellency, and I too am a different person! He is unique, and I am unique; really, I am quite unique." But when he stands before the eminent man, he becomes embarrassed and begins to stutter and to talk so senselessly that His Excellency and his guests become uneasy. The physician who is present, the same whom Golyadkin had consulted, observes him especially sharply. His double, who enjoys His Excellency's favor, is naturally also there and finally throws him out.

After Golyadkin has waited for a long time concealed in the courtyard of Klara's house, pondering once more all the pros and cons of his plan, he is suddenly discovered from the brightly lit windows and is invited most charmingly—by his double, of course—into the house. Believing that his intention has been discovered, he is prepared for the worst; but quite to the contrary, he is received kindly and politely by everyone. A happy mood comes over him and he feels full of affection, not only for Olssuf Ivanovich, but for all the guests—even for his dangerous double, who appears altogether no longer as evil, not even as the double, but rather as a completely ordinary and amiable person. Nonetheless, the hero gets the impression from the guests that something special must be brewing. Thinking that it concerns a reconciliation with his double, he offers his cheek for a kiss. But it seems to him "as if something evil emerged in the ignoble face of Mr. Golyadkin the Younger—the grimacing kiss of Judas. . . . There was a roaring in Mr. Golyadkin's ears, and all became dark before his eyes. It seemed that an endless file of Golyadkin-images were rushing very noisily through the door into the room." Actually, a man does unexpectedly appear at the door, the sight of whom inspires our hero with horror, although he "had earlier already known everything and sensed something similar." It is the doctor, as the triumphant double maliciously whispers to him.

The doctor takes away the pitiable Golyadkin, who endeavors to justify himself to the people present and who gets into a carriage with him, which immediately moves off. "Shrill, completely unrestrained screams from his enemies followed him in farewell. For a while, several forms kept up with the vehicle and gazed inside. Little by little, however, they became fewer, until they finally disappeared and only Mr. Golyadkin's impudent double remained." The double runs alongside the carriage now to the left, now to the right, and blows kisses as adieux. He too disappears at last, and Golyadkin becomes unconscious. He revives in the darkness of night beside his companion and learns from him that he will receive free board and lodging since he is traveling for the government. "Our hero uttered a cry and seized his head between his hands—so that was it, and he had suspected it all along!"

Apart from the figure of the double, which takes the form of various types, all these tales exhibit a series of coinciding motifs so noticeable that it seems hardly necessary to call special attention to them once again. We always find a likeness which resembles the main character down to the smallest particulars, such as name, voice, and clothing—a likeness which, as though "stolen from the mirror" (Hoffmann), primarily appears to the main character as a reflection. Always, too, this double works at cross-purposes with its prototype; and, as a rule, the catastrophe occurs in the relationship with a woman, predominantly ending in suicide by way of the death intended for the irksome persecutor. In a number of instances this situation is combined with a thoroughgoing persecutory delusion or is even replaced by it, thus assuming the picture of a total paranoiac system of delusions.

Taking notice of these typical traits shared by a succession of writers is aimed not so much at proving their literary interdependence—in some cases just as positive as it is impossible in others—as at calling attention to the identical psychic structure of these authors, which we now intend to consider somewhat more closely.

III

Biography as Background to Literature

> After all, poets are always Narcissi.
> A. W. SCHLEGEL

> Love for oneself is the beginning of a lifelong novel.
> OSCAR WILDE

> Love for oneself is always the beginning of a novelistic life . . . for only when one's ego has become a task to be assumed, does writing have any meaning.
> THOMAS MANN

It is not our purpose to investigate pathographically, or even analytically, the lives and works of the writers with whom we are here concerned. We intend only to show that a cross-section through one particular stratum of their psychic constitution might reveal the complex consistencies in certain characteristic features, from which result identical psychic reactions.

The chief trait shared by those writers in whom we are interested is apparent enough: they, like some others of similar nature, were decidedly pathological personalities who, in more than one direction, went beyond even that limit of neurotic conduct otherwise allowed to the artist.[1] They suffered—and obviously so—from psychic disturbances or neurological and mental illnesses, and during their lifetimes they demonstrated a marked eccentricity in behavior, whether in the use of alcohol, of narcotics, or in sexual relations—with particular emphasis in the latter case upon the abnormal.

We know that Hoffmann, whose mother was a hysterical personality, was nervous, eccentric, and strongly dependent upon moods. We know too that he suffered from hallucinations, delusions of grandeur, and compulsive ideas—all of which he was fond of portraying in his writings.[2] Afraid of becoming insane, he "often thought he saw before him his living mirror-image, his double, and other spectral figures in disguise" (Klinke, p. 49). When he was writing about them, he actually saw around him the doubles and horrifying shapes; and, when working at night, he often anxiously awakened his wife in order to show her these forms (Klinke, p. 174).[3] After one drinking bout, he wrote in his diary: "Seized by thoughts of death: doubles" (Hitzig, I, 174, 275). At the age of forty-seven he succumbed to a neurological illness, which Klinke diagnosed as chorea but which was also considered to be paralysis. At any rate, either disease gives evidence of his neuropathic constitution, which he shared with most of his companions in adversity whom we still have to discuss.

1. Similar authors, we suggest, are Villiers de l'Isle-Adam, Baudelaire, Strindberg, Kleist, Günther, Lenz, Grabbe, and Hölderlin.

2. See Otto Klinke, *Hoffmanns Leben und Werke vom Standpunkt eines Irrenarztes* (2nd ed.; Braunschweig and Leipzig, 1908), p. 6 and *passim;* [Richard von] Schaukal, "E. T. A. Hoffmann," in *Die Dichtung* (Berlin, 1904), Vol. XII, and the sources there cited, especially Hitzig's recollections [J. E. Hitzig, *Aus Hoffmanns Leben und Nachlass* (2 vols.; Berlin, 1823).]

Psychiatric and occult literature, with which Hoffmann was well acquainted, provided him with additional inspiration for his themes. He is said to be indebted particularly to [Gotthilf Heinrich] Schubert's books, which were widely read at that time. *Die Symbolik des Traumes* (Bamberg, 1814) states that the feeling "of a double personality is perceptible to the somnambulist, and also after long illnesses; it is actually present at moderate intervals in insanity and in the dream" (p. 151).

3. In Maupassant's *He*, the main character takes a wife in order to be protected from such peculiar sensations.

So it was with Jean Paul, who likewise was afraid of becoming insane and who contended with severe psychic traumas in his struggle toward creative expression. A central factor in his psychological conflicts is his relationship to his ego. His biographer Schneider points out in detail the significance of this for Jean Paul's mental disorders and for his literary characters: "Jean Paul relates, as one of the most noteworthy remembrances from his childhood, that the insight 'I am an I' came to him as a boy like a flash of lightning; and since then, it remained a shining image before him. . . . During his stay in Leipzig, that powerful perception of his own self forced itself upon him like a terrifying specter" (Schneider, p. 316). In 1819, the writer enters into his diary: "First of all, [I must record] this incident: I am looking at Örthel one night in Leipzig, after a serious conversation; he is looking at me; and both of us shudder upon becoming aware of our Self." (Schneider, p. 316). "In *Hesperus*, he causes his ego to assume the uncanny form of a spirit before him, the effect of which is that of a basilisk. We already see that the writer is occupied in artistically reproducing his delusional fancy, a fancy of which he cannot rid himself. Over and over again he loses himself in the contemplation of his own ego in solitude. . . . From the ego, the primitively perceived absolute within the swirling fluctuations of relationships (*The Invisible Lodge*), that ego gradually emerged which, at one time a transparent and trembling dream-figure, stands beside his own ego; at another time and as a mirror-image, it rises up threateningly, moves toward the glass, and is about to step forth. Jean Paul carries this terrible idea on and on" (Schneider, pp. 317–18). We have already traced the artistic expression of these ideas.

In the same breath with Hoffmann, one is accustomed to mention Edgar Allan Poe, whose life was just as eccentric as his writings.[4] Here too, as with Hoffmann and Jean Paul, we find unfavorable conditions in the parental home. Poe lost his parents at the age of two and was brought up by relatives. In puberty he experienced a severe depression upon the death of the mother of a much-admired comrade. Also about this time he be-

---

4. Hanns Heinz Ewers, *Poe* (Berlin, 1905); H. Probst, "Poe," in *Grenzfragen der Literatur und Medizin*, ed. S. Rahmer (Munich, 1908), fasc. 8. [See also Marie Bonaparte's classic *Edgar Poe, étude psychanalytique*, Paris, 1933; *The Life and Works of Edgar Allan Poe: A Psycho-analytic Interpretation*, tr. John Rodker, London, 1949.]

gan to use alcohol, later on habitually drinking to excess and turning to opium approximately the last ten years of his life. At twenty-seven, he married his cousin, hardly fourteen years old. She died some years later of consumption, a disease to which his parents had also succumbed, and his first attack of delirium tremens occurred soon after his wife's death. A second marriage did not take place because he overindulged himself in alcohol on the day before the wedding and then left town.[5] In the year of his death he established a relationship with a woman, now a widow, whom he had loved in his youth. His death, occurring at only thirty-seven [forty] years of age, apparently resulted from delirium tremens.

Along with traits of character which are typical of alcoholism and epilepsy, Poe gives evidence of phobic reactions (especially to being buried alive) and of neurotically compulsive brooding (cf. the stories *Berenice, The Tell-Tale Heart*, etc.). His pathographer Probst calls him a feminine personality and emphasizes the asexuality of his fantasies—"he lacked the ability for sexual love"—a deprivation which Probst considers to be the result of overindulgence in alcohol and opium. In addition, he describes Poe as being egocentric: "His whole mind revolves only around his ego" (Probst, p. 25). The story *William Wilson* is generally considered to be a personal confession. In it Poe also describes someone who, in gambling and drinking, deteriorates more and more until he finally destroys himself in defiance of his better self.

The life and sufferings of Maupassant are similar, even though more poignantly tragic.[6] Like Hoffmann, he too was the product of a decidedly hysterical mother and was doubtless strongly predisposed to his mental illness, which was brought about through an external cause.[7] Where Poe's dissipations were alcoholic, those of Maupassant were amorous. Zola says of him: "He was a dreaded Lothario who always brought back from his expeditions the most amazing tales about wenches—all sorts of impossible erotic adventures at the narration of which our good

5. In his perceptive essay on Poe, Baudelaire psychologically explains this incident by the fact that the author wanted to remain faithful to his first wife, for this reason provoking the breach of engagement.

6. Paul Mahn, *Maupassant* (Berlin, 1908); Gaston Vorberg, "Maupassants Krankheit," in *Grenzfragen des Nerven- und Seelenlebens*, ed. L. Löwenfeld (Wiesbaden, 1908), fasc. 60.

7. His disposition to mental illness is confirmed by the fact that his younger brother Hervé met his end through paralysis.

friend Flaubert would laugh so hard that his eyes filled with tears." When Maupassant, at about the age of twenty-eight, complained to Flaubert that he could no longer get pleasure from women, his friend wrote to him: "Always women, you little swine. . . . Too much whoring around, too much straining at the oars, too much physical activity . . ." (Vorberg, p. 4). Actually, he was an energetic, healthy person at this time, eager for adventures and having a really fabulous capacity for work.[8] In his thirtieth year, however, the first signs became apparent of the progressive paralysis which overcame the writer thirteen years later. His once anecdotal and delightful stories, often abounding in earthy sensuality, gradually give way to gloomy confessions, predominated by a mood of intense moroseness. His book *Afloat* (1888) expresses these circumstances of his life in the form of a diary.

Little by little, Maupassant resorted to all kinds of narcotic agents and, with their help, does seem to have gained a temporary control over himself. Indeed, according to his own statement, several of his works were written under the influence of such agents—an assertion which has been made also in the cases of Poe, Hoffmann, Baudelaire, and others. And, like these authors, Maupassant too—though from a different cause—suffered from hallucinations and illusions and often described them in his works. Later on, he produced a series of interesting delusional images, had notions of megalomania and persecution, and also made an attempt at suicide.

Long before this, he had struggled against his "inner enemy," whom he has so splendidly presented in *The Horla*. This story, along with *He* and much else, is nothing but a deeply stirring description of himself. He recognized early and clearly the cleft in his personality: ". . . because I bear within me that double life which is the strength, and simultaneously the misery, of the writer. I write because I feel; and I suffer from everything which exists because I know it only too well; and above all, because I see it in myself, in the mirror of my thoughts, without being able to experience it" (*Afloat*, entry for April 10).

Like Poe, Maupassant also has a pronounced egocentric orientation ("I am very quickly wearied by everything that does not come to completion in me"); and, despite his intensive

---

8. "From 1880 to 1890, aside from numerous newspaper articles, he wrote sixteen volumes of short stories, six novels, and three volumes of travel descriptions" (Vorberg, *op. cit.*, p. 5).

sexual life, he never did find in love the right relationship to woman: "a happiness which I did not know and which, in quiet foreknowledge, I held to be that which is most sublime on earth" (*Afloat*). Women especially cause him to feel clearly his inability for real devotion: "Most of all, the women let me perceive that I am alone. . . . After every kiss, after every embrace, my feeling of isolation is more enhanced. . . . Yes—even in those moments which seem to reveal a mysterious understanding, when wish and longing blend and one imagines that one has descended into the depths of her soul—a word, one single word, exposes our error and shows us, like a flash of lightning on a stormy night, the abyss between both of us" (*Solitude*). Just as here, bound to his ego, he is unable to attain to the woman's self, so in *He* does he flee from this uncanny and terrifying ego to the woman.

That Maupassant's psychic *schisma* was objectified directly by the imagining of a double is shown by a hallucination, reported by Sollier, which the author "experienced one afternoon in 1889 and related that same evening to a trusted friend. He was sitting at the desk in his study. His servant had strict orders never to enter while his master was working. Suddenly, it seemed to Maupassant as if someone had opened the door. Turning around he sees, to his extreme astonishment, *his own self entering*, who sits down opposite him and rests his head on his hand. Everything Maupassant writes is dictated to him. When the author finished his work and arose, the hallucination disappeared" (Vorberg, p. 16).[9]

Other writers also experienced similar apparitions of themselves. The most familiar incident is probably the episode in Sesenheim related by Goethe (at the close of Book II, Part 3, of his autobiography *Fiction and Truth*) in which he takes leave of Friederike and rides along the footpath toward Drusenheim. ". . . then one of the strangest premonitions came over me. I saw myself—not with my real eyes, but those of my mind—riding on horseback toward me on the same road and clothed in a garment such as I had never worn: its color was the gray of a pike, with some gold in it. As soon as I roused myself from this dream, the figure had completely disappeared. It is strange, however, that after eight years I found myself on this same road, going to visit Friederike once more, wearing the garment of which I had dreamed and which I was wearing not from choice, but by accident. Whatever may be the state of affairs in these matters, the curious optical illusion did afford me some comfort in those moments of parting. The pain of leaving forever the magnificent

9. See Paul Sollier, *Les phénomènes d'autoscopie* (Paris, 1913).

Alsace, along with everything I had gained there, was mollified. . . ."
If the lover's wish not to be compelled to forsake his beloved is
without any doubt the impulse causing this self-apparition,[10] then
similar hallucinations, in various other situations, are reported by
Shelley.[11]

It is noteworthy that Chamisso, the author of *Peter Schlemihl*,
also gave artistic form to a similar incident of seeing one's
second self. In that work he describes how he comes home at
midnight after carousing and finds his room occupied by his
double (as Maupassant has described the same situation in *He*,
Dostoyevsky in *The Double*, Kipling, and others).[12] Now a
quarrel arises between them as to who is the genuine occu-
pant.[13] The author accounts for himself as one who has always
aspired toward the beautiful, the good, and the true, while his
double boasts of cowardice, hypocrisy, and selfishness. Chamisso,
acknowledging with shame that his double is his true self, retreats in defeat.

Like most of the works which we discuss, Chamisso's *Peter
Schlemihl* is generally recognized as an avowedly autobiographical work: "Peter Schlemihl is Chamisso himself, 'whose

10. Freud has told me conversationally that he interprets the appearance
in strange garb as an excuse to justify disloyalty, making it possible for him
to attain other goals (the costume of officialdom).

11. [J. E.] Downey, "Literary Self-Projection," *Psychological Review*,
XIX (July, 1912), 299.

12. In *Wilhelm Meister*, too, the Count thinks that he sees his double
sitting at his desk and is so deeply shaken by this experience that his whole
demeanour changes. He becomes melancholy and thinks only of death.

> A terrifying vision came: I see,
> Appalled, my Self beside my desk am standing.
> I cry: "Who art thou, ghost?"—At once cries he:
> "Who rouses me so late at spirits' hour?"
> And, turning pale as I, he looks at me.

[Chamisso, "Erscheinung" (1828), ll. 20–24, in *Chamissos Werke*, ed.
O. Walzel, *DNL*, CXLVIII, 289–290.]

13. Cf. the presumption of the shadow in Andersen's fairy tales. The
confrontation of the double-image as a personification of one's own evil impulses—as an attempt to form an ethical contrast—is especially evident in
the cases of double-consciousness (R. L. Stevenson, *Doctor Jekyll and Mr.
Hyde*). It is also present in Dostoyevsky's Golyadkin and is indicated in
The Student of Prague. In Poe's *William Wilson* the double seeks to play
the part of a guardian angel, or admonisher. Chamisso's lines read:

> In all its truth my Self shall be apparent,
> Illusion's veil to nothingness dissolved!

[Chamisso, "Erscheinung," ll. 41–42.]

characterization is really my own,' he says in a letter to Hitzig."[14]
This statement is corroborated not only by Schlemihl's external
appearance and by many aspects of his personality, but also by
the other characters, who have unmistakable models in the
author's life. Bendel was the name of his valet; the coquettish,
vain, and pleasure-craving Fanny has her prototype in Ceres
Duvernay, the author's beautiful but egotistic compatriot, who
for years caused him both happiness and unhappiness;[15] and
the devoted, dreamy Mina recalls Chamisso's brief idyl with
the poetess Helmina von Chezy. Some light, too, is cast upon
the personal roots of the story by the anecdote mentioned
by Chamisso as being its genesis. He writes in a letter: "I had
lost on a journey my hat, valise, gloves, handkerchief, and all
movable belongings. Fouqué asked whether I had not also lost
my shadow, and we imagined how it would be if this misfortune had really happened."[16] This scene clearly shows that the
bungling and timid Chamisso, even in the circles of his friends,
was considered to be a "schlemiel."[17]

14. See Ludwig Geiger, "Chamisso," in *Dichter und Biographien* (Leipzig, 1907), Vol. XIV; *Aus Chamissos Frühzeit: Ungedruckte Briefe und
Studien* (Berlin, 1905). See also Fr. Chabozy, *Über das Jugendleben Chamissos zur Beurteilung seiner Dichtung Peter Schlemihl* (diss., Munich,
1879).

15. In a letter Chamisso takes Ceres to task about her egotism: "My dear
sister, your sad egotism and false pride are faults which I have occasionally
reproached very strongly and which I must still reproach, because they
alarm me, and it is I whom they are able to offend" (Chabozy, *op. cit.*,
p. 7, n.).

16. On another occasion, as told by a friend, the poet and Fouqué went
for a walk in sunlight at a time when the small Fouqué's shadow appeared
almost as large as that of the tall Chamisso. The latter is said to have
threatened in jest to roll up his companion's shadow.

17. Chamisso writes on March 27, 1821, to his brother Hippolyt about the
name "Schlemihl": "Schlemihl—or, better, Schlemiel—is a Hebrew name,
meaning Gottlieb, Theophil, or *aimé de dieu*. In Jewish colloquial language
it refers to clumsy and unfortunate people who are never successful in anything. A schlemiel breaks off a finger in his vest-pocket, falls on his back
and breaks his nasal bone, and always shows up where he is not wanted.
The schlemiel, whose name has become proverbial, is a person of whom the
Talmud tells the following story: one is having relations with a rabbi's wife,
lets himself be caught in the act, and is slain. This is a good illustration of
the plight of the schlemiel, who has to pay so dearly for that which everyone else gets away with."
Heine (*Romanzero*, Book III, fourth poem) illustrates this ultimate misfortune even more drastically: Pinchas, intending to stab Simri, who was
making love to a woman, struck the completely innocent schlemiel instead.
Some derive the name from 'schlimm mazzel,' which means 'unfortunate
destiny' (see *The Jewish Encyclopedia*). According to [F. E.] Anton,

That he himself was aware of being such a person is plainly evident from the poems "Misfortune" and "Patience," both from the year 1828, when he was almost fifty years old. In these poems, the poet says that the beginnings of his "unhappiness" appeared in his childhood. The year of his marriage (1819) also produced the poem "Adelbert [Adalbert] to His Bride," which shows the great solace that the poet, as a reward for his many renunciations, had finally found in love. In a letter of June in the same year, he also congratulates himself upon having found a loving bride and not having become a "schlemiel." He himself, therefore, makes the connection between this trait and a defective ability to love, just as the rest of his main characters, in the conceit of their egotism, are incapable of sexual love. A concomitant vanity also can be attributed to Peter Schlemihl, who concludes his narrative with the advice to his creator: " . . . If you intend to live among men, learn to respect first of all their shadows, and only then their money. *If you want to live only for yourself and for your better self—* oh, in that case, you need no advice." Walzel, too, stresses the moral of the story: that man in due course should struggle for the realization "that he has need only of himself alone in order to be happy" [*Chamissos Werke*, ed. Oskar Walzel, in *Deutsche Nationalliteratur* (Stuttgart, 1892–1893), CXLVIII, lviii].

We must take into account the striking fact that so many of the writers whom we consider here met their wretched ends from severe neurological or mental illnesses. They include Hoffmann, Poe, and Maupassant as well as Lenau, Heine, and Dostoyevsky. In observing this fact—primarily only as far as it has the meaning of a special dispositional character—we must not overlook the circumstance that this trait usually comes to the surface oftentimes prior to the eruption of the individual's destructive sufferings, and that it also takes other forms. Thus Lenau was restless, disgusted with life, melancholy, and dejected.[18] Heine, too, suffered from moodiness and neurotic conditions before being overcome by his grave neurasthenia, the paralytic nature of which has recently again been doubted. It

---

Wörterbuch der Gauner- und Diebssprache ([2nd ed.] Magdeburg, 1843), p. 61, the name is from the language of roguery and meant 'unlucky person' (as is well known, the argot of criminals contains many Jewish elements).

18. See the psychographical study of J. Sadger, ["Aus dem Liebesleben Nicolaus Lenaus"], in *Schriften zur angewandten Seelenkunde*, ed. Sigmund Freud (Vienna, 1910), fasc. 6.

is characteristic of his deeply rooted duality in thought and emotions that he early recognized it. We have already noticed it in Jean Paul's childhood experience of his ego; and Heine, Musset, and others report it of themselves. In his memoirs Heine speaks of having undergone as a boy a kind of personality-alteration and of having believed that he was living the life of his great-uncle.[19] And Musset confesses that ever since his boyhood a sharply outlined duality had moved through his inner life.[20] The clear form which this duality assumed in the course of time is shown by the poem we have discussed in which the double appears on all significant occasions. In his *Confessions of a Child of His Century*, the poet describes his peevish moods as well as his attacks of rage (*accès de colère*), the first of which he experienced, at the age of nineteen, from jealousy of his sweetheart.[21] These fits of jealousy later recurred, especially in his relationship with the older George Sand—a liaison which the couple themselves termed "incestuous." After this affair broke up, Musset, who even prior to it had been frivolously inclined, gave himself over to drinking and sexual excesses, thus prematurely ruining himself both psychologically and physically.

This succession of pathological authors may be concluded with two of them who had definitely critical neurotic symptoms. There is no doubt that in the case of Ferdinand Raimund an unfavorable predisposition is a factor, just as it appears in those writers who were mentally disturbed. Raimund, however, suffered predominantly from moods of acute bad temper, melancholia, and hypochondriacal fears—all of which eventually drove him to suicide.[22] Ever since adolescence, he demonstrated extreme irritability, flashes of anger, mistrust, etc., as well as suicidal impulses and attempts, which in the course of years led to grave emotional trouble. In his autobiographical sketch, Raimund states: "Because of the constant mental and physical strains and vexations of life, I became the victim in

19. "There is nothing more uncanny than seeing one's face accidentally in a mirror by moonlight" (Heine, *Die Harzreise*).

20. See the poet's biography by his brother Paul; see also Paul Lindau, *Alfred de Musset* (2nd ed.; Berlin, 1877).

21. In his first volume of poems, which he published at the age of eighteen, Musset dealt almost exclusively with the themes of adultery, disloyalty, and duels between the rivals in these matters, of whom one always dies.

22. Cf. J. Sadger, "Friedrich Raimund, eine pathologische Studie," in *Die Wage* (biannual issue 1; Vienna, 1898), fasc. 13–25.

1824 of a serious nervous malady, which almost turned into consumption." He thought that he was deceived by false friends; outbursts of rage alternated with deep melancholic resignation; and insomnia entered the picture. Most likely, his unhappy marriage, soon terminated by divorce, contributed to all this.

The divorce seems to be the final point in a series of unhappy amorous episodes, for again and again the writer succumbed to this passion, fatal to his well-being, but which, as he himself said, had a very strong control over him. Nor was his last, great love for Toni completely happy. He, however, felt that the fault was his own and that he was fundamentally incapable of love.[23] This realization may have been a principal reason for his carrying out the impulse to suicide which lay dormant in him and which used an external cause (the fear of rabies) only as a rationalization. Years before his violent end, clear signals of a deep disturbance were already evident. In 1831 the playwright said to the novelist [Karl] Spindler: "Something deep and evil dwells within me that is undermining me; and I assure you that my comic successes were only too often born of thorough desperation. Often people cannot tell by looking at me what a sad jester I am."[24]

Raimund became more and more exacting, mistrustful, and melancholic. To his earlier fears was added that of losing his voice, weak as it was anyway. His condition at that time—four years before his death—was already such that [Carl Ludwig] Costenoble entered into his diary: "That man will either go mad, or kill himself." In the year of his death, Raimund's hypochondriacal and apprehensive fears reached an intolerable peak: "Even at 7:30 in the evening he closed all doors and shutters securely; and even the postman, who had an important message

23. Raimund says in *Album-Leaf* (1834):
    I am lonely even 'mid the bustle,
    Though I long to be where men repair,
    Lonely even in the madding hustle,
    Who'll his joys, his pleasure with me share?
    Those I once knew well are now as strangers,
    And, since thou art gone, I have but gall,
    Pain, and ceaseless brooding on death's dangers,
    Melancholy shrouds me like a pall.
    Certes do such thoughts attempt to blandish,
    But alas! my peace fore'er is vanish'd:
    Canny servants hold their lord in thrall.
24. [Eduard] Castle (ed.), *Raimunds Werke* [Leipzig, 1903], p. cix. For other biographical details, see Wilhelm Börner, "Friedrich Raimund," in *Dichter und Biographien* (Leipzig, 1905), Vol. XI.

to deliver to him, was unable to persuade him to open the door.
From this time on, he also never left the house without a pistol"
(Börner, p. 91). "Overcome by fear and anxiety, he often locked
himself in during his last weeks of life and did not even want
to see his sweetheart" (Castle, p. cxi). When his dog accidentally bit him during this time, the delusion of getting hydropho-
bia (which had come to the surface ten years earlier) seized
him, and he put an end to his life.[25]

These pathological traits make it possible for us to understand
the opinion that *The King of the Alps and the Misanthropist* offer
the clearest self-portrait of its author. Grillparzer, upon whose advice Raimund intended to treat this theme once again, stressed
that the playwright "had been able to copy himself a little in the
strange main character."[26] More positive is Sauer's opinion: "Here
Raimund could play himself, put himself on the stage; Raimund
himself was the model for his Rappelkopf ['grouch']; through
this imaginative copy, he sought to rid himself of his own morbid moods."[27] This statement is corroborated by the "Resignation"
after the first production of the play (October 17, 1828) which,
aside from other references, speaks of the role thus:

> Those moods malign, which did upon me weigh,
> Through this, my part, have lightly passed away:
> Disdain, mistrustful anger's agitation,
> Avenging rage, from life—no consolation,
> Disgrace, remorse—*in fine,* boundless torments. . . .[28]

There can also be no doubt about Dostoyevsky's severe mental illness, even though the diagnosis (epilepsy) is debatable.[29]

25. The effect of this bite could perhaps have a connection with the fact
cited by Castle (*op. cit.,* p. xl) that the author had been bitten on a finger
by his fiancée during an argument just before their wedding ceremony. The
marriage ended in divorce.

26. He intended to present, instead of a mere change of characters, a
change in the *basic conception* of the theme. This project, which was to be
entitled "A Night on the Himalaya," never materialized (Börner, *op. cit.,*
p. 71).

27. August Sauer, ["Ferdinand R. Raimund"], in *Allgemeine Deutsche
Biographie* (Leipzig, 1888), XXVII, 736–54.

28. Besides Rappelkopf and *The Spendthrift* (already cited), Raimund
also split the personality of Wurzel (*The Millionaire Peasant*), confronting
the man simultaneously with his youth and his old age. This motif of senes-
cence will receive our attention later on. We may add a characteristic touch
from Raimund's boyhood: the future actor "stood for hours before the mirror, grimacing at himself and trying to stretch his mouth widely, so that also
in this regard he might resemble his image" (Börner, *op. cit.,* p. 9).

29. See, more recently, Jolan Neufeld, *Dostojewski: Skizze zu seiner
Psychoanalyse* (Leipzig, Vienna, and Zürich, 1923).

Even at an early age he was odd, and his mode of life was marked by shyness and withdrawal. Like Raimund, he was extremely mistrustful and considered everything done to him as an affront and as purposing to insult and vex him.[30] As a youth in engineering school, according to his own statement, he is said to have had mild seizures (of an epileptic nature)—like those of Poe, with whom he also shared the fear of being buried alive. In any case, the assertion that his illness broke out for the first time in his banishment seems unfounded.[31] On the contrary, Dostoyevsky himself says that his illness disappeared from the moment of his arrest and that he suffered not one seizure during the entire term of his sentence. His wife writes in her notebook that, according to his own words, he would have become insane if this catastrophe had not occurred [cf. *Dostoyevsky Portrayed By His Wife: The Diary and Reminiscences of Madame Dostoyevsky*, tr. and ed. S. S. Koteliansky (New York, 1926)]. This circumstance, psychologically easy to understand, does seem, however, rather to speak for a hysterical ailment (with pseudo-epileptic seizures). These seizures took place with great frequency and intensity after the writer's return to social life. In his works he has very often described them masterfully.[32] Dostoyevsky himself says of his seizures: "For a few moments I feel such a happiness as is impossible in one's normal condition and of which others can have no conception. . . . This sensation is so strong and so sweet that one could give away ten years of his life, or the whole of it, for the bliss of a few such seconds." After the seizures, however, he was quite depressed, feeling himself to

30. Tim Segaloff, M. D., "Dostojewskis Krankheit," in *Grenzfragen der Literatur und Medizin*, ed. S. Rahmer (Munich, 1907), fasc. 5.

31. In *Tolstoi und Dostojewski* [tr. Carl von Gütschow] (Leipzig, 1903), pp. 77 ff., Dmitri Merezhkovsky makes an observation of significance for the infantile origin of the illness: "In any case, it is very probable that the strict morality of the father, his surliness, his tendency to flare up in anger, and his deep mistrust, all had a deep [sic] influence on Fedor Michailovich. . . . Only one of Dostoyevsky's biographers raises the curtain concealing this family secret just a little, but he immediately lets it drop back. In mentioning the origin of Dostoyevsky's epilepsy, he remarks very reservedly and obscurely: 'There still exists a very special story about Fedor Michailovich's illness—a story which traces this illness to a *tragic event in his earliest childhood* taking place within his family; but, although I have heard this from a person who was very close to Fedor Michailovich, I have never obtained confirmation of this rumor from any source. For this reason, I have decided not to set it forth in precise detail.'"

32. Cf. Merezhkovsky, *op. cit.*, pp. 241, 243; cf. also N. Hoffmann, *F. M. Dostojewski: eine biographische Studie* (Berlin, 1899), p. 225.

be a criminal; and it seemed to him as if some unknown guilt were burdening him.[33] "I have a seizure every tenth day," he writes in the last days of his stay in St. Petersburg, "and then I don't come to my senses for five days; I am a lost man." "My reason really suffered; that is the truth. I feel this, for my wrecked nerves brought me, now and then, close to insanity."[34]

In his behavior, he was eccentric in every direction—"in gambling, in lascivious debauches, in searching for mystic terrors" (Merezhkovsky, p. 84). "Everywhere and always," he writes of himself, "I have gone to the ultimate limit; and in all my life, I have gone beyond that limit without fail." In characterizing him, we must add that he—eccentric like Poe—was also filled with an exalted self-esteem and opinion of himself. In his adolescence (at about the time he was finishing *The Double*), he writes to his brother: "I have a terrible vice: a boundless love of myself, and ambition." His pathographer says that he was the amalgam of all varieties of self-infatuation.

Vanity and egotism are also typical of many of his fictional characters, such as the paranoiac Golyadkin, one of his earliest creations. The author lent many traits of his own personality (also characteristic of his later works) to Golyadkin and repeatedly termed him his "confession" (Hoffmann, p. 49).

Merezhkovsky (pp. 273–74) sees the double-motif in Dostoyevsky's works as a central problem: "So with Dostoyevsky all the tragic, struggling couples among his most vividly real characters—who appear to one another as unified, whole beings—turn out to be actually only the two halves of a third, cloven entity, who mutually seek and pursue each other as doubles." About Dostoyevsky's artistic morbidity, he says: "In fact, what sort of peculiar artist is he who, with insatiable curiosity, pokes around only in the diseases, only in the most terrible and disgraceful abscesses of the human soul? . . . And what sort of oddities are these 'blissful ones,' these possessed persons, fools, idiots, crackpots? Perhaps he is not so much an artist as a doctor of mental illnesses, withal a doctor to whom one would have to say, 'Physician, first heal thyself'" (Merezhkovsky, p. 237).

So clear is the close psychological relationship between the literary personalities whom we have sketched that, in recapitulating, we need call special attention only to its basic structure. The

33. Merezhkovsky, *op. cit.*, p. 92.
34. *Ibid.*, p. 113.

pathological disposition toward psychological disturbances is conditioned to a large degree by the splitting of the personality, with special emphasis upon the ego-complex, to which corresponds an abnormally strong interest in one's own person, his psychic states, and his destinies. This point of view leads to the characteristic relationship (which we have described) to the world, to life, and particularly to the love-object, to which no harmonious relationship is found. Either the direct inability to love or—leading to the same effect—an exorbitantly strained longing for love characterize the two poles of this overexaggerated attitude toward one's own ego. The various forms taken by the theme we have been treating are similar even down to slight details. The predilection for this theme—beyond any literary indebtedness or influences—becomes psychologically comprehensible through these striking and extensive conformities in the nature, and in the individual traits of character, of the type we have described.

But the typically-recurring basic ways in which these forms appear do not become intelligible from the writer's individual personality. Indeed, to a certain degree they seem to be alien to it, inappropriate, and contrary to his way of otherwise viewing the world. These are the odd representations of the double as a shadow, mirror-image, or portrait, the meaningful evaluation of which we do not quite understand even though we can follow it emotionally. In the writer, as in his reader, a superindividual factor seems to be unconsciously vibrating here, lending to these motifs a mysterious psychic resonance. The purpose of the following section is to use ethnographic, folkloric, and mythological traditions to demonstrate the part played by ethnopsychology and to relate it to those individually revived features which have the same meaning. The section also intends to prepare us to notice the common psychological basis of the superstitious and artistic representations of these impulses.

IV

The Double
in Anthropology

Man's shadow, I thought, is his vanity.

NIETZSCHE

Our point of departure will be those superstitious notions associated with the shadow which even today are encountered among us and which writers—for example, Chamisso, Andersen, and Goethe—could consciously utilize.

Quite generally known in all of Germany, Austria, and Yugoslavia is a test made on Christmas Eve or New Year's Eve: whoever casts no shadow on the wall of the room by lamplight, or whose shadow is headless, must die inside of a year.[1] There is a similar belief among the Jews that whoever walks by moonlight in the seventh night of Whitsuntide, and whose shadow is head-

1. Th. Vernaleken, *Mythen und Bräuche des Volkes in Österreich* [Vienna, 1859], p. 341; [Otto Frh. von] Reinsberg-Düringsfeld, *Das festliche Jahr* [in *Sitten, Gebräuchen und Festen der germanischen Völker* (Leipzig, 1863)], p. 401; A Wuttke, *Der deutsche Volksaberglaube* [*der Gegenwart*, ed. E. H. Meyer (3rd ed.; Berlin, 1900)], II, 207, 314.

less, will die that same year.[2] There is a saying in the German prov-
inces that stepping upon ones own shadow is a sign of death."[3]
Contrasting with the belief that whoever casts *no* shadow must
die is a German belief that whoever sees his shadow as a duple
during Epiphany must die.[4] Various theories, some of them rather
complicated, have been offered to explain this idea. We shall
single out the one referring to the belief in a guardian spirit.[5]

From this shadow-superstition, some scholars believe, developed the belief in a guardian spirit, which in its turn is closely related to the double-motif.[6] Rochholz [see n. 2] takes the shadow
following his [*sic*] body to be the original content of the stories
about second sight, visions of oneself, the shadow in the armchair, the double, and the apparition lying in one's bed.[7] As time
passes, the shadow which survives the grave becomes the double
which is born with every child.[8] Pradel [see n. 3] finds an explanation for the belief in the disastrous effect of the duple
shadow in the idea that one's guardian angel appears at the hour
of death and joins one's shadow.[9] Here lies the root of the idea
important to our theme: that the double who catches sight of
himself must die within a year.[10] Rochholz, who has especially

2. E. L. Rochholz, "Ohne Schatten, ohne Seele. Der Mythus vom Körper-
schatten und vom Schattengeist," *Germania*, V (1860), [69–94], contained
in the same author's *Deutscher Glaube und Brauch* [*im Spiegel der heidnischen Vorzeit*] (Berlin, 1867), I, 59–130 (quotations). About Jewish
shadow-traditions specifically, cf. [M.] Gaster, ["Zur Quellenkunde deutscher Sagen und Märchen"], *Germania*, XXVI (1881), 210.

3. Wuttke, *op. cit.*, p. 388. In Silesia and Italy it is said that in such cases
one no longer grows; cf. Fritz W. Pradel, "Der Schatten im Volksglauben,"
Mittlg. d. Schles. Ges. f. Volksk., XII (1904), 1–36 [1–37?].

4. Wuttke, *op. cit.* Among the Slovaks the same is true for Christmas
Eve; cf. J. v. Negelein, "Bild, Spiegel und Schatten im Volksglauben,"
Arch. f. Rel.-Wiss., V (1902), 1–17.

5. Pradel, *op. cit.*; Rochholz, *op. cit.*

6. See E. H. Meyer, *Germanische Mythologie* (Berlin, 1891), pp. 62,
66 ff. In Modern Greek, 'shadow' is used directly in the sense of protective
spirit; cf. Bernhard Schmidt, [*Das*] *Volksleben der Neugriechen* [*und das
hellenische Alterthum* (Leipzig, 1871)], I, 169, 181, 199, 229, 244.

7. Heino Pfannenschmid, [*Germanische Erntefeste im heidnischen und
christlichen Cultus mit besonderer Beziehung auf Niedersachsen*
(Hannover, 1878)], p. 447, was the first to object to this explanation, which
was felt by several to be too one-sided.

8. Negelein, *op. cit.*

9. Pertinent here is the Grimm fairy tale (number 44) about "Godfather
Death," whom the hero successfully escapes by lying in bed in reverse
position (cf. also the note in Vol. III).

10. Adolf Bastian, *Ethnische Elementargedanken in der Lehre vom
Menschen* (Berlin, 1895), p. 87; Wuttke, *op. cit.*, p. 212; Rochholz, *op. cit.*,
p. 103; [Otto] Henne am Rhyn, "Kultur der Vergangenheit [in verglei-

been concerned with the belief in guardian spirits, thinks that the meaning of such spirits as beneficient was the original one and that only gradually did their harmful (death) meaning develop along with the strengthening of the belief in a life after death.[11] "So an individual's shadow, which in his lifetime had been a helpful attendant spirit,[12] must shrivel into a terrifying and persecuting specter that torments its protégé and chases him unto death" (Rochholz [see n. 2]).[13] How extensively this occurs will become clear in the psychological discussion of the whole topic.

These superstitious notions and fears of modern civilized nations concerning the shadow have their counterpart in numerous and widespread prohibitions (taboos) of savages which refer to the shadow. From Frazer's rich collection of material, we realize that our "superstition" finds an actual counterpart in the "belief" of savages.[14] A large number of primitive peoples believe that every injury inflicted upon the shadow also harms its owner (Fra-

chender Darstellung]," in *Gegenwart und Zukunft* (Königsberg, 1892), I, 193. According to Wuttke (p. 49), the expression "second sight" originally had the meaning of a double's sight; whenever the person sees himself, however, he must die in the course of a year. Cf. Villiers de l'Isle-Adam, *Das zweite Gesicht* [Berlin, 1909].

11. Rochholz, *op. cit.*, pp. 128 ff. According to him, 'shadow' later became equivalent with 'harm' (Schatten = Schaden); i.e., taken synonymously with 'black; on the left; false; not at liberty; damned'; [these German words do not have the same etymological origin].

12. In German antiquity, Rochholz distinguishes three kinds of the protective spirit, which correspond to the three ages of man and to the three times of day—visible by the respective shadow—and which seem to have some sort of relationship to the Norns. With the Nordic belief, "Whoever sees his *fylgja*, him it abandons, and he loses his life thereby," Rochholz makes interesting references to the legends of the Staufenberger, of Melusine, The White Lady, Orpheus, and so on. The love affair of this *fylgja* with her body leads to other problems, such as the mystical concept of the soul as bridegroom and similar ideas. About the belief in a protective spirit, cf. F. S. Krauss, *Yreća, Glück und Schicksal im Glauben der Südslawen* (Vienna, 1888).

13. A widespread locution, "to fear one's shadow," is frequently used by writers. Cf. here the painful fear of Maeterlinck's "Princess Maleine" at the sight of a shadow. Further, in R. Stratz' *Foolish Virgin* (p. 307), we find: "You are afraid of yourself and are running away from yourself like the man who quarreled with his shadow." Pradel, from whom these references are taken, cites in connection with this the expression σκιαμαχεῖν from Plato (*Apol.* 118 D, *Republic* 520). In Strindberg's *Inferno. Legends*, a passage reads: " 'I believe you are afraid of your own shadow,' laughed the physician contemptuously" (p. 228).

14. James G. Frazer, "The Soul as a Shadow and a Reflexion," *The Golden Bough: Taboo and the Perils of the Soul* (3rd ed.; London, 1911–1915), III, 77–100.

zer, p. 78), thereby opening wide the door to necromancy and magic. It is noteworthy that in some of the literary works we have discussed an echo of magical influence can be recognized in the death of the main character at the wounding of his reflection, portrait, or double.[15] According to Negelein, "the attempt to destroy persons by wounding their doubles is widely known, even from antiquity" [sic]. Also, according to Hindu belief, one destroys an enemy by stabbing his picture or shadow in the heart (Oldenberg, Veda, p. 508 [see n. 80]).[16]

Primitive peoples have no end of special taboos relating to the shadow. They take care not to let their shadows fall upon certain objects (especially foods); they fear even the shadows of other people (especially pregnant women, mothers-in-law, etc.; see Frazer, pp. 83 ff.); and they pay heed that no one steps upon their shadows. On the Solomons, east of New Guinea, every native who steps upon the King's shadow is punished with death (Rochholz, p. 114). The same is true in New Georgia (Pradel, p. 21) and among the Kaffirs (Frazer, p. 83). Primitive peoples are also especially careful not to let their shadows fall upon a corpse or its grave, and for this reason funerals very often took place at night (Frazer, p. 80).

The meaning of death in all these events is reduced to the fear of illness or other harm. Whoever casts no shadow, dies; whoever has a small or faint shadow is ill, while a well-outlined shadow indicates recovery (Pradel). Such tests for health were really made,

15. This relation also finds an echo in the Germanic legal custom of the so-called "expiation by the shadow," according to which, e.g., a serf insulted by a freeman takes revenge on the latter's shadow (literature in Rochholz, p. 119; see also Jakob Grimm, Deutsche Rechtsaltertümer (4th ed.; Leipzig, 1922), pp. 677 ff.). In Emperor Maximilian's time, the punishment for having "cut off" a shadow with a spade was severe. A passage in Luther's "Table Talk" refers to this (Pradel, pp. 14 ff.), as does a tale by Hermann Kurtz in Erzählungen (Stuttgart, 1858) Vol. I. This expiation by the shadow, quite seriously intended, appears in isolated Oriental traditions with an ironic emphasis upon its worthlessness (cited by Pradel, op. cit., p. 23). In the Bahar Danush (Benfey, Pantschatantra, I, 127), a youth's shadow is to be whipped on the complaint of a maiden whose image in a mirror he has kissed. To King Bokchoris of Egypt, the wisest judge of his time, was attributed the famous judgment which sent a complaining courtesan, whose charms a lover had enjoyed in a dream, to the shadow, or to the reflected image, for the amount to be paid for amends (Plutarch, Demetrius, 27); Erwin Rohde, in Der griechische Roman und seine Vorläufer (3rd ed.; Leipzig, 1914), 370, 1 [sic], sees in this the model for the lawsuit about the donkey's shadow (cf. Wieland's Die Abderiten; cf. also Robert Reinick, Märchen-, Lieder- und Geschichtenbuch (Bielefeld, 1873).

16. For greetings and curses applicable to the shadow, see Oldenberg, p. 526, n. 4.

and many peoples even nowadays carry the sick out into the sunlight in order to lure back their expiring souls with their shadows.
With the opposite intention, the inhabitants of Amboyna [Am-
boina, Ambon] and Uliase, two islands on the Equator, never
leave their houses at noon, because in this location their shadows disappear and they are afraid of losing their souls along with
them (Frazer, p. 87). Relevant here are the notions about the
short and the long shadows, the small and the lengthening ones,
on which Goethe's[17] and Andersen's fairy tales are based, as is
the poem by Stevenson-Dehmel. The belief that the health and
strength of a person increase with the length of his shadow
(Frazer, pp. 86 f.)[18] pertains here, just as does the distinction
of the Zulus between the long shadow of a person, which becomes an ancestral spirit, and the short, which remains with the
deceased.

Attached to this belief is another superstition, associated with
the rebirth of the father in the son. Savages who believe that the
soul of the father or grandfather is reborn in the child fear, according to Frazer (p. 88), too great a resemblance of the child
to his parents.[19] Should a child strikingly resemble its father, the
latter must soon die, since the child has adopted his image or sil-
houette. The same holds for the name, which the primitive views
as an essential part of the personality. In European culture the
belief is still retained that if two offspring of the same family
bear the same name, one must die.[20] We recall here the same
"nomenphobia" in Poe's *William Wilson* and can also understand,
on the basis of "name magic," the invocation of spirits by calling
their names.[21]

17. Strikingly similar to the shadow-motif in Goethe's tale is a story
from South America told by Frazer (*op. cit.*, p. 87): "The Mangaians
[*sic;* Mangaia is one of the Cook Islands in Polynesia] tell of a mighty
warrior, Tukaitawa, whose strength waxes and wanes with the length of
his shadow." At last, a hero discovers the secret of Tukaitawa's power (the
Samson-theme) and slays him at noon, when his shadow is slightest.

18. So believe the Bagandas of Central Africa and the Kaffirs in South
Africa. In Solothurn, the greater or less intensity of the shadow was con-
sidered as a criterion of health (Walzel, introduction to Chamisso's works,
Deutsche Nationalliteratur, Vol. CXLIX).

19. J. v. Negelein, "Ein Beitrag zum indischen Seelenwanderungs-
glauben," in *Arch. f. Rel.-Wiss.*, 1901. See also Frazer, "The Belief in
Immortality and the Worship of the Dead," *Among the Aborigines of
Australia* . . . (London, 1913), I, 92, 315, 417.

20. Henne am Rhyn, *op. cit.*, p. 187.

21. For the prevention of magical customs, the Jews forbade the mention of the name "Jehova." See Friedrich Giesebrecht, *Über die alttest.
Schätzung des Götternamens* [*und ihre religionsgeschichtliche Grundlage*]

According to Freud, all tabooed objects have an ambivalent character, and signs pointing to this are also not lacking in shadow-concepts. The ideas of rebirth of the paternal shade in the child, just pointed out, lead to the already-mentioned notions of the shadow as a protective spirit born simultaneously with the child. In direct contrast to the ideas of death in shadow-superstition are the ideas—even though much less current—of the shadow as a fecundating agent (Pradel, pp. 25 f.). The image of the shadow of death surrounding mankind finds its opposite Biblical expression in the Annunciation, which promises Mary, though virginal, a son, for δύναμις ὑφίστου ἐπισχιάσει σοι ("the power of the Most High shall overshadow thee," Luke 1:15 ["virtus Altissimi obumbrabit tibi," Luc. 1:35]).

We note that St. Augustine and other patristic fathers see in the expression ἐπισχιάσει the concept of coolness as the opposite to sensual procreation. Pradel relevantly cites the expression, "Just be quiet; you aren't overshadowed by the Holy Spirit." From this basis he adduces a Tahitian myth, according to which the goddess Hina becomes pregnant from the shadow of a breadfruit tree which her father Taaroa shook.[22] The taboos of the mother-in-law's shadow, which Frazer cites, are obviously intended to prevent such an impregnation by means of a shadow.[23] Thus, for example, among the natives of South Australia a ground for divorce occurs when the husband's shadow accidently falls upon his mother-in-law. In Central India there is a general fear of being impregnated by a shadow, and pregnant women avoid contact with a man's shadow since it might cause her child to resemble him (Frazer, "The Belief . . . ," p. 93). When we compare these fancies with those of the increasing and decreasing

---

(Königsberg, 1901). Giesebrecht shows that the name, the shadow, and the soul are identical in popular belief (p. 79) and explains that the name becomes a threatening double of the person (p. 94). Concerning the taboo of names, cf. Freud, "Totem und Tabu," *Ges. Schriften,* IX; and concerning its effect in our unconscious, cf. Freud, "Zur Psychopathologie des Alltagslebens," *Ges. Schriften,* IV.

22. After Rehsener in *Zeitschrift d. Vereines f. Volksk.,* VIII, 128; cf. Georg Waitz, *Anthropologie der Naturvölker,* VI, 624 f., who sees in this the remnant of the old Tahitian belief that the moon, which resembles breadfruit, copulates during the new moon.

23. Frazer, "The Belief . . . ," p. 83 ff. Frazer himself believes, moreover, that the "avoidances" in the relationship of mother-in-law and son-in-law could arise from the fear of incest (p. 85, n. 6). Freud has given the psychoanalytical confirmation and extension of this view (*Totem und Tabu*).

shadow and with the correspondingly variable virility (the Samson motif), the symbolic representation of the shadow for male potency becomes evident. In its turn, it is related to one's own regeneration in descendants, and hence to fertility.

Similar to Lenau's ballad "Anna," the concept of the shadow's fertility is also the basis of Richard Strauss' opera *The Woman without a Shadow*. The opera was derived from an Oriental source, and Hugo von Hofmannsthal wrote the libretto. Its focus is upon an Oriental princess [*sic*] whose father has incurred a terrible guilt. The guilt can be expiated (so prophesies a red falcon to the princess on her wedding day) only if there is prospect of her bearing a child within three years of the marriage. The years pass but the princess's wish remains unfulfilled—she is a woman without a shadow. At the close of the third year, the red falcon reappears and grants a respite of five days. In this emergency, the nurse makes use of a ruse: she finds a young dyer who yearns for the blessing of children, refused him by his quarrelsome wife. Corresponding to a belief current in Eastern legends, the nurse intends to purchase this woman's shadow—i.e., fertility—in return for costly treasures and for a lover quickly and illusively conjured from a wisp of straw. From the fire on the hearth, the voices of the unborn children—who, in the shape of little fishes, have been placed magically through the window and into the frying-pan—sound a warning lament (reminiscent of a Grimm fairy tale). The Empress feels a deep, humane sympathy for the poor woman, whom she does not want to deprive of a point of destiny which signifies the essence of female delight. In this moment of spiritual purgation a marvelous light encloses her, and the longing of her heart becomes reality. She, the shadowless woman who formerly was as transparent as crystal, suddenly casts a shadow; and Richard Strauss causes the mystical chorus of the unborn children to sound forth from higher spheres.

Just as almost all symbols of good fortune were originally fertility symbols, the shadow, too, has gained a meaning of good fortune from this aspect. Not only the curative effect of the shade of certain trees (especially in the Bible) is pertinent here, but above all the role of the shadow as the guardian of treasure (cf. Pradel)—indeed, even as the augmenter of it (practically, too, the shadow functioned as the marker of property boundary lines). In the Indic fairy tale of the woodcutter's daughter, the spirit wooing the poor girl says to her father: "Give me your daughter; then shall your shadow grow, and your treasures shall become great" (Rochholz, after the fairy tale collection of the *Somadeva Bhatta*). We are reminded here of Peter Schlemihl, the student Balduin, and others who are recompensed for the loss of their shadows by wealth. They intend to use this wealth to gain the beloved girl, but they fail miserably.

Nor are the heroes of similar literary creations any more successful when the problem of the double takes the form of the exchange of physiques (the Amphytrion motif)—for example, in Théophile Gautier's short story *The Soul-Exchange*. The particular interest of this story lies in its placing the wish for rejuvenation into the foreground. Octave, who falls into a protracted illness from his unrequited love for someone else's wife, obtains from his aged physician the soul of his troublesome rival, hoping in this way to gain a hearing with the wife. She, however, recognizes the deception and remains cool toward him. Her husband challenges Octave to a duel and Octave kills him; but, tormented by conscience, he goes again to the old doctor, who now transfers his own soul into the body of the young man. Octave's soul in its turn vanishes into the senile body of the doctor.

These motifs emerge with particular force in Jules Renard's grotesque novel *Doctor Lerne*, the main character of which undertakes to solve the problem anatomically and surgically by inverting the personality through an exchange of brains. Old Lerne, who has been rejected by Emma, the embodiment of sexuality, assumes the young body of his nephew in order to be loved by Emma as much as the robust youth. His project, however, meets with as little success as in Gautier's short story. The duel with the double appears here in this way: the "nephew," magically placed into the body of a bull, almost slays his physical identity (with another brain); he is jealous because it is embracing Emma, the creature of sexuality. This extreme step is prevented only by the uncle's interrupting the remarkable duel between the animal and human self. At the critical moment he exclaims: "Dear friend, by doing that you will kill yourself!"

In these, as well as in several other developments of the double-motif, a particular accent is placed upon the theme of impotence. In many cases the impotence is adduced as a motivation for the physique-exchange and for the rejuvenation associated with it. In other cases it easily betrays this tendency—for example, in Arthur Schnitzler's short story *Casanova's Return Home*. In this story the aging hero purchases a *nuit d'amour* with a beautiful and coy woman from her youthful lover, who externally resembles Casanova in his youth.

The idea early appeared in psychoanalytic circles of interpreting Schlemihl's lack of a shadow as impotence,[24] and Robert Hamerling's *Homunculus* [1888] (Book V) seems to allude to this idea: ". . . Peter Schlemihl; the well-known 'man' (the worst-off!) without a shadow. . . ." Wilde's fairy tale "The Young Fisherman and His Soul" (in *The Pomegranate House*) would fit in with the castration meaning of the loss of shadow. The hero wants to get rid of his soul, which stands between him and his beloved mermaid, and with a knife cuts off his shadow. His life finally ends, like that of Dorian Gray, in suicide.

We turn now from such individually distinct meanings of the double and shadow in their obviously symbolistic-sexual sense to the more comprehensive problem of that image which has been constructed by one's guardian spirit into a pursuing and torturing conscience, well founded in the traditions of folklore. Folklorists are in agreement in emphasizing that the shadow is coequivalent with the human soul. From this fact we derive not only the particular regard for the shadow, but also for all taboos referable to it and for superstitious fears of death after stepping upon it, since injury, harm, or loss of one's soul will bring about

---

24. There has been much controversy about the meaning of Schlemihl's shadow, and the literature about it is rather large; cf. Julius Schapler, *Chamisso-Studien* (Arnsberg, 1909). The shadow was claimed to be an allegorical representation of the fatherland, position in life, the family, the home area, religious adherence, orders and titles, human respect, social talent, and so on; and correspondingly, the loss of the shadow meant the lack of these things. Even in the lifetime of the author, who was skeptical toward all of these interpretations, the shadow is said to have been interpreted, with his agreement, as the individual's external honor ([Karl Joseph] Simrock, [*Handbuch der deutschen Mythologie mit Einschluss der Nordischen*], 4th ed. [Bonn, 1874], p. 482). This would, however, by no means prevent its having other—and unconscious—meanings, of which Chamisso himself has provided several. Because it reminds us of popular superstition, the following comment by the author is of interest. He is said to have made it to a friend a few weeks before his death: "People have so often asked what the shadow might be. Indeed, if they were to ask what my shadow is now, I would say that it is my lack of health; my lack of a shadow consists of my illness." The quote is from Franz Kern, *Zu deutschen Dichtern* (Berlin, 1895), p. 115. In the concluding section of this book it will be apparent to what extent the sexually symbolic interpretations can be subsumed under a more inclusive psychological understanding. Impotence and other interpretations are cited in Sadger, "Psychiatrisch-Neurologisches in psychoanalytischer Beleuchtung." *Zentralblatt f. d. Gesamtgeb. d. Medizin* (1908), Nos. 7 and 8.

death. We quote Tylor[25] on the identification of the shadow with the soul among primitive peoples, including the most undeveloped natives of Tasmania:

> So the Tasmanian used his word for 'shadow' simultaneously to mean 'spirit'; the Algonquins call a person's soul 'his shadow'; in the Quiché language *nahib* serves for 'shadow, soul'; the Arawak *neja* means 'shadow, soul, image'; the Abiponians had only one word, *loákal*, for 'shadow, soul, echo, image.' . . . The Basutos not only call the spirit which remains after death the *seriti*, or 'shadow,' but they believe that when someone walks along the river bank, a crocodile could seize his shadow on the water and draw it down; and in Old Calabar we find this same identification of the spirit with the shadow, the loss of which is very dangerous for one.[26]

According to Frazer, certain natives of Australia assume also the existence, apart from the soul localized in the heart (*ngai*), of a soul very closely associated with the shadow (*choi*).[27] Among the Massim in British New Guinea the spirit, or the soul, of a deceased person is called *arugo*, equivalent in meaning with 'shadow' or 'reflection.'[28] The Kai in Dutch New Guinea consider their souls, or parts of them, to be in their reflections and shadows; therefore, they are careful not to step upon their shadows.[29] In North Melanesia the word *nio*, or *niono*, means both shadow and soul.[30] Among the Fiji Islanders the term for 'shadow' is *yaloyalo*, a reduplication of the word for 'soul,' *yalo*.[31] Incidental to noticing that the natives of the Strait of Torres islands use the word for spirit, *mari*, at the same time for 'shadow,' or 'image,' Frazer thinks that many uncivilized peoples derived their denomination for the human soul from observing shadows or the reflection of the body in water.[32]

A series of further folkloric investigations has shown without any doubt that primitive man considered his mysterious double, his shadow, to be an actual spiritual being:

> That man in the Cameroons naturally meant his shadow, when he said, "I can see my soul every day: I simply place myself toward the sun" (Mansfeld). So Spieht reports of the people of Ewe: "The person's soul can be seen in his shadow." J. Warnek of the Bataks: "They believe that their shadows embody their individual souls."

25. Tylor, *Primitive Culture* [3rd. ed.; London, 1891], I, pp. 423 ff.
26. Adolf Bastian, *Vorstellungen von der Seele*, pp. 9 f. [?].
27. Frazer, "The Belief in Immortality . . . ," p. 129.
28. *Ibid.*, p. 207.   29. *Ibid.*, p. 267.
30. *Ibid.*, p. 395.   31. *Ibid.*, p. 412.
32. *Ibid.*, p. 173.

Klamroth of the Saramos: "The shadow cast by a living person becomes a *kungu* (spirit) by uniting with the soul of the deceased; for
the soul (*mayo;* anatomically also 'heart') disintegrates, but the
shadow does not disintegrate." Guttmann of the Jagga Negroes:
"What remains of the deceased, and descends into the realm of the
dead, is his shadow, *kirische.* This is not just a figure of speech for
the personality deprived by death of a body, but rather it means quite
literally the person's shadow as it is cast upon the earth by sunlight.
The same concept is found among the Salish and Dénés in Canada's
Far West."[33]

The Fiji Islanders believe that every person has two souls—
a dark one which exists in his shadow and goes to Hades, and a
bright one which exists in his reflection on the surface of water
or in glass and which remains nearby his place of death.[34] From
this meaning of the shadow, the numerous precepts and prohibitions (taboos) relating to it can be sufficiently well understood.

If we ask how it came about that the shadow was taken to be
the soul, the views of primitive peoples living with nature—as
well as the views of ancient civilized peoples—are of help toward an answer: that the primordial concept of the soul, as
Negelein puts it, was a "primitive monism" in which *the soul fig-
ured as an analogon to the form of the body.* So the shadow,
inseparable from the person, becomes one of the first "embodi-
ments" of the human soul, "long before the first man saw his reflection in a mirror" (Negelein). The belief of primitive peoples
all over the world in the human soul as being an exact copy of
the body, first perceivable in the shadow,[35] was also the original
soul-concept of ancient civilized peoples. Erwin Rohde, probably
the most sensitive observer of the belief in the soul and of its
cult in Greece, says: "The belief in the psyche was the oldest and
very first hypothesis by which one explained the apparitions of
dreams, of fainting, and of ecstatic vision by assuming a special

33. Quoted after G. [Gerhard] Heinzelmann, *Animismus und Religion*
. . . ([Gütersloh], 1913), pp. 18 f.
34. Frazer, "The Belief in Immortality . . . ," p. 411. Similar views of
two souls among the Greenlanders and Algonquins are reported by Paul
Radestock, *Schlaf und Traum* (Leipzig, 1878 [1879]), p. 252, n. 2. The
Tamis in German New Guinea also distinguish between a long, motile
soul identified with the shadow, and a short one, which leaves the body
only at death (Frazer, "The Belief . . . ," p. 291).
35. The rather undeveloped North-Melanesians, among whom the terms
for 'soul' and 'shadow' are formed from the same linguistic root (see
above), "think that the soul is like the man himself" (Frazer, "The Belief . . . ," p. 395); and "the Fijisan pictured to themselves the human
soul as a miniature of the man himself" (*ibid.,* p. 412).

physical agent in these obscure actions. Already in Homer we can note the path in the course of which the psyche evaporates into a mere abstraction."[36] "According to the Homeric conception, man has a twofold existence: in his perceptible presence, and in his invisible image which only death sets free. This, and nothing else, is his psyche. In the living human being, completely filled with his soul, there dwells, like an alien guest, a *weaker double*, his self other than his psyche . . . whose realm is the world of dreams. When the other self is asleep, unconscious of itself, the double is awake and active."[37] "Such an eidolon and second self, duplicating the visible self, has originally the same meaning as the *genius* of the Romans, the *fravauli* of the Persians, and the *Ka* of the Egyptians." In Egypt, too, the shadow was the oldest form of the soul (Negelein according to Maspero); and according to Moret[38] there were alternate terms for soul, double (*Ka*), image, shadow, and name.[39] By referring to a copious literature, Spiess also supports the belief of savages in the continued existence of a shadow-like soul after death (p. 172 [see n. 37]); and he also cites the meaning of the Hebrew expression "Rephaim" for what remains of man after death: "the weary or the feeble ones, i.e., the shadows, the inhabitants of the Underworld, a name analogous to the Greek term" (p. 422).

The most primitive belief in the soul is therefore linked with death, as Spiess has shown for civilized peoples, and as Frazer ("The Belief . . .") has especially shown for the most undeveloped savages. The first concept of the soul among primitives,

36. Erwin Rohde, *Psyche: Seelencult und Unsterblichkeitsglaube der Griechen* (3rd ed., Tübingen, 1903), I, 6 ff. and 46. Similar material about the Greenlanders and other peoples is found in Radestock, *op. cit.*, chap. 1 and its annotations.

37. Cf. the Homeric concept of the soul as the shadow ($\epsilon\iota\delta\omega\lambda\upsilon$) of the once living person (*Iliad* xxiii. 104; *Odyssey* x. 495; and xi, 207). Achilles, to whom the slain Patroclus appears in a dream, exclaims: "Ye gods, then there is really within the portals of Hades a psyche and a shadow of man!" See also Edmund Spiess, *Entwicklungsgeschichte der Vorstellungen vom Zustande nach dem Tode* (Jena, 1877), p. 283. According to Spiess, after death the $\psi\upsilon\chi\eta$, the soul, which is identical with the spirit, becomes an $\epsilon\iota\delta\omega\lambda\upsilon$, i.e., a shadow, a dream-image (*Odyssey* xi. 222).

38. Alexandre Moret, *Annales du Musée Guimet* (Paris, 1902), Part 14, p. 33.

39. Also, the practice of embalming the dead, particularly among the Egyptians (but also elsewhere—see Spiess, *op. cit.*, pp. 182 f.; and Frazer, *op. cit.*, pp. 144 ff.), as well as the custom of placing gifts into the grave (food and fire for the souls) point to the fact that originally the soul was imagined to be very material and equal to the body.

which is significant for the entire development of human history, is that of the spirits of the deceased imagined in most instances as shadows, just as even today we speak of the "realm of shades" of departed ones.

Since the souls of the deceased are shadows, they themselves cast no shadows—a condition which the Persians, for example, asserted directly of those again brought back to life.[40] Indeed, according to several authors, the observation that the corpse no longer casts a shadow is said to have lent support to the assumption that the soul had escaped in the shadow.[41] Thus the Arcadian sacred region of Lykaion, in which a complete lack of shadows prevails, was considered to be the realm of those initiated into death.[42] According to Pausanias, *Description of Greece* (VIII, 38, 6), the entrance into this region was denied to mankind, and whoever transgressed the law necessarily had to die within a year's time. Here, therefore, as in almost all of the cited superstitious ideas, the lack of a shadow indicates approaching death, the absence of whose shadow is anticipated. Thus, according to Rochholz (p. 19), in the Lycaic abaton "the protective daimon retreats from the consecrated intruder and abandons him to the terrors of death."[43]

Not only the souls, but also the spirits, elves,[44] daimons, ghosts, and magicians[45] closely associated with them have no shadows, because they originally are themselves shadows, i.e., souls. For this reason, spirits and elves, considered to be shadowless by New Zealanders, accept nothing offered to them except

40. Spiess, *op. cit.*, p. 266. In Dante's *Purgatory*, the "shades" also cast no shadows. Rohde says of the immortality of these souls: "They live scarcely no more than does the image of the living person in the mirror."

41. Negelein, *op. cit.*; Herbert Spencer, *Prinzipien der Soziologie*, tr. into German by B. Vetter [Stuttgart, 1877–1897], II, 426.

42. [Friedrich Gottlob] Welker, *Kleine Schriften* [Bonn, 1844–67], III, 161, refers to the belief of the Pythagoreans, who took literally the locution, "getting rid of one's shadow." In accordance with their view the dead person's soul casts no shadow. In Arcadia this was a euphemistic expression for death (cf. our 'umschatten') and only later was this expression taken literally. Concerning the various ideas of this cultic lack of a shadow, cf. W. H. Roscher, "Die Schattenlosigkeit des Zeus Abatons auf dem Lykaion," in *Fleckeisens Jahrbuch für klassisches Altertum*, CXLV (1892), as well as the literature cited there, especially Karl Otfried Müller, *Die Dorier* (Breslau, 1824), I, 308.

43. Concerning the human sacrifices held in the Lycaic sacred place, see Negelein, *op. cit.*

44. [Rochholz, *op. cit.*, p. 75.]

45. Negelein, *op. cit.*

the shadow.[46] The high-born damsel is recognized by the fact that she casts no shadow, because she is a spirit. The devil, according to a Russian belief (Gaster), also has no shadow because he is an evil spirit, and for this reason is he so eager for human shadows (cf. the pact by Schlemihl, Balduin, and others). Whoever has come under the devil's influence casts no shadow (Pradel). The numerous legends in which the devil is cheated of his reward by receiving "only" the shadow instead of the soul which was his due[47] appear to represent a too-serious reaction upon the loss of a shadow. Originally—as Schlemihl and his successors demonstrate—it may have been mankind who was deceived in this case, since man underestimated the shadow, the value of which was known to the devil.[48]

From abundant folkloric material of civilized peoples, Negelein has shown that "the superstitious ideas and customs deriving from the *mirror image* resemble in all their chief features those produced by the shadow-image." Also prominent in this connection are the apprehensions of death and of misfortune. In German territories the prohibition exists of placing the corpse before a mirror or of looking at it in a mirror; for then two corpses appear, and the second one foretells a second incident of death.[49] Ac-

46. Waitz, *op. cit.*, pp. 297, 300.

47. See Jakob Grimm, *Deutsche Mythologie* (4th ed.; Berlin, 1875–1878), pp. 855, 976, and the note on p. 302; Karl Victor Müllenhoff, *Sagen, Märchen und Lieder der Herzogthümer Schleswig-Holstein und Lauenburg* (Kiel, 1845[?]), pp. 554 ff. About the Spanish legend of the devil of Salamanca, which Theodor Körner treated in a romance, cf. the sources in Rochholz, *op. cit.*, p. 119; the poem itself is in *Deutsche Nationalliteratur*, CLII, 200. In Salamanca, the devil was giving instructions to seven pupils, of whom the last had to pay with his soul. Once, however, he pointed to his shadow with the remark that it would be the last to leave the room. The devil took the shadow, and the pupil remained shadowless and unhappy for the rest of his life.

48. This is shown by the traditions in which the devil directly stipulates the shadow as the pay for his aid—(see, e.g., Konrad Maurer, *Isländische Sagen* [*Isländische Volkssagen der Gegenwart* . . . (Leipzig, 1860)], p. 121)—or in which a person whom the devil has somehow cheated must be without a shadow for the rest of his life (see Müllenhoff, *op. cit.*, p. 454 f.; Grimm, *Deutsche Mythologie*, p. 976). The tradition cited by Rochholz (p. 119) is interesting, according to which a Count Villano ('scoundrel'), who had given over his shadow to the devil, learned from him the art of rejuvenating old people (rejuvenation-motif) and wanted to apply it to himself. In old age, therefore, he had himself killed, cut into pieces, and these parts placed into a glass which was buried in horse manure. This was prematurely discovered, however, and the not yet completely developed child was burned (on this theme cf. Herbert Silberer's essay, "Homunculus," *Imago*, III (1914), 37–79.

49. Wuttke, *op. cit.*, pp. 435 ff.

cording to a Dalmatian superstition, also found in Oldenburg, whoever sees himself in a mirror will die as long as there is a corpse in the house.[50]

The general applicability of this fear is apparent from the frequency of its contrary measure, which requires the veiling of mirrors so that the soul of the deceased person may not remain in the house. This custom is practised today in Germany and France and among the Jews, Lithuanians, and others.[51] Since the soul of the departed person is thought to be in the mirror, it can become visible there under certain circumstances. In Silesia it is said that at midnight on New Year's Eve, if one takes two burning lights in front of a mirror and calls the name of a deceased person, that person will appear in the mirror.[52] In France one's reflection is said to be glimpsed in a mirror as one will appear at the hour of death, if previously on the eve of Epiphany a certain ceremony is carried out.[53]

These ideas are associated with the prohibitions of gazing at oneself in the mirror at night. If this is done, one loses his own image—i.e., one's soul. As a result, death is a necessary consequence,[54] an idea based in East Prussia upon the belief that in such cases the reflection of the devil appears behind one. If, in fact, anyone notices the reflection of another face beside his own, he will soon die.[55] For similar reasons it is disastrous for ill and asthenic persons to see their reflections,[56] especially according to a Bohemian belief.[57] In all of Germany the falling down

50. Karl Haberland, "Der Spiegel im Glauben und Brauch der Völker," *Zeitschrift für Völkerpsychologie*, XIII (1882), 324–47. Cf. also Riess, *Rhein. Mus.* (1894), LIX, 185.

51. Haberland, *op. cit.*, p. 344. According to Frazer, *op. cit.*, p. 95, this is true also in Belgium, England, Scotland, Madagascar, and among the Jews in Crimea and the Mohammedans in Bombay. The reasoning is that the soul of the survivor, reflected in a mirror, could be taken away by the spirit of the dead person which is staying in the house.

52. Haberland, *op. cit.*

53. *Ibid.*

54. *Ibid.*, pp. 341 ff., after Grimm's *Deutsche Mythologie*, appendix, *Deutscher Aberglaube*, no. 104; Friedrich Wilhelm Panzer, *Beiträge zur deutschen Mythologie: Studien zur germanischen Sagengeschichte* (Munich, 1910), II, 298; Ludwig Strackerjan, *Aberglaube und Sagen aus dem Herzogtum Oldenburg* (2nd ed.; Oldenburg, 1909), I, 262; Wolff-Mannhardt, I, 243; IV, 147[?]; J. N. Ritter von Alpenburg, *Mythen und Sagen Tirols* (Zürich, 1857), p. 252; Wuttke, *op. cit.*, p. 205.

55. Wuttke, *op. cit.*, p. 230.

56. Negelein, *op. cit.*

57. Haberland, *op. cit.*; Frazer, *op. cit.*, p. 95.

or breaking of a mirror is taken to be a sign of death,[58] although along with that, and as a euphemistic compensation, seven years of trouble are in prospect.[59] Also, whoever's last view of himself was in a broken mirror must die[60] or suffer seven years of distress.[61] If thirteen people are sitting together, whoever is sitting opposite a mirror must die.[62] In order to obtain protection from the mysterious forces of the mirror, a cat is reflected in a new mirror in certain regions.[63] Precautions, too, are taken against allowing small children to gaze at themselves in a mirror. These precautions result from the fear of one's own reflection, which subjects one's double to all kinds of harm;[64] and if the child is not protected, he will become proud and frivolous or else will become ill and die.[65]

According to Negelein, the conviction that the mirror reveals concealed matters is based upon the belief in a double. This reference includes, first of all, the magic use of the mirror in order to discern the future. So in Oldenburg, for example, it is said that one can see his future in a mirror by stepping in front of it at midnight with two burning lights, gazing attentively into it, and calling one's name thrice. In association with the customs we have cited, it is clear here that "whether," not "what," is meant by "future"; that is, what is of primary interest to the individual is his own lifespan. In contrast, the significance of the mirror as a prophet of love diminishes, although a girl, in practicing similar customs, generally sees her "intended one" (equivalent, to her, with "the future").[66] Vain girls, however, see the devil's face when they look into the mirror at night,[67] and if they smash a mirror, they think that they will not be married for seven years.

We shall omit the magical and mantic applications of the mirror and water reflections (reported by Negelein and Haberland [see n. 50]) and shall pass directly to its origin among primitive

58. Haberland, *op. cit.*

59. Wuttke, *op. cit.*, p. 198.

60. *Ibid.*, p. 404.

61. Ibid., p. 198.

62. Haberland, *op. cit.*

63. Negelein, *op. cit.*

64. *Ibid.*

65. Wuttke, *op. cit.*, pp. 368 f.; see also Weber's *Demokritos*, IV, 46.

66. Wuttke, *op. cit.*, pp. 229 f., 234; Haberland, *op. cit.* E. T. A. Hoffmann also repeatedly used this popular belief in his writings; see K. Olbrich, "Hoffmann und der deutsche Volksaberglaube," in *Mitteilungen der Gesellschaft für Schlesische Volkskunde* (1900). F. S. Krauss, in "Urquell," deals with the mirror-superstition associated with the "nights of Andreas."

67. Negelein, *op. cit.*

peoples.[68] Savages believe that the soul is embodied in the image reproduced by glass, water, portrait, or by a shadow.[69] This belief relates to the numerous taboos attached to these objects.[70] In a tribe in Dutch India, adolescent children must not look into a mirror because it is thought that it will deprive them of beauty and cause ugliness.[71] Zulus do not look into a dirty swamp, since it casts no reflection. They believe that a monster dwelling there has taken the reflection away, so that they have to die. When someone dies among the Basutos without obvious cause, they believe that a crocodile has submerged his reflection.

The similarly based dread of one's own portrait or of a photograph is found all over the world, according to Frazer.[72] It is present among the Eskimos, the American Indians, and tribes in Central Africa, as well as in Asia, East India, and Europe. Since these people visualize the person's soul in his image, they fear that the foreign possessor of this image can have a harmful or deadly effect upon it. Many savages actually believe that death is imminent if their picture is taken or is in the possession of a stranger. Frazer relates delightful stories of the savages' fear of photography, as does, more recently, the missionary Leuschner of the Yaos in South China.[73] This fear of one's own image, because

68. Cf. the essay on "Spiegelzauber" by G. Róheim, *Imago*, V (1917–1919), 63–120, which is based upon abundant folkloric material; cf. also his book of the same title in the *Internationale Psychoanalytische Bibliothek*.

69. Thomas Williams, who lived among the Fiji Islanders, tells the following story which is characteristic for the psychic meaning of the mirror-image: "I once placed a good-looking native suddenly before a mirror. He stood delighted. 'Now,' said he softly, 'I can see into the world of spirits.'" (after Frazer, "The Belief . . . ," p. 412.)

70. Frazer, "The Belief . . . ," pp. 92 ff.

71. *Ibid.*, p. 93. Kleist, who treats the problem of the double in *Amphytrion*, gives the psychological basis of this superstition in his remarks "On the Puppet-Theatre." Here he tells of a handsome and well-educated youth who, in order to imitate the pose of the "Boy Extracting Thorn From Foot," began to stand all day long before the mirror; and continually one charm after the other left him . . . and when a year had passed, not one trace of loveliness could be discovered in him." Cf. here the legend of Entelidas and the favorite novel character of Dorian Gray; [see pp. 18, 67].

72. Frazer, "The Belief . . . ," pp. 96–100.

73. Leuschner, *Mitteilungen der Geographischen Gesellschaft zu Jena* (1913). Concerning similar material on the Malay Archipelago, cf. *Zeitschrift für Ethnologie*, XXII, 494 f. According to [Carl] Meinhof, *Afrikanische Religionen* (Berlin, 1912), the recording of the voice with the phonograph occasionally meets with similar difficulties.

of the belief in the soul, overlaps every figurative representation. Meinhof says: "A plastic representation of a human being can disturb the African very much; and it has happened that the work of art had to be destroyed in order to tranquilize the excited person" [in most of West Africa plastic art is *usually* in the form of human beings]. Warneck reports of the Waschambas that they did not want to be alone with the photographs of human beings which the missionaries had put up in their room; they feared that the pictures could come alive and approach them.[74]

A German superstition has it that one may not allow one's portrait to be painted;[75] otherwise one will die.[76] Frazer has traced the same belief in Greece, Russia, and Albania, and he gives evidence of its traces in modern England and Scotland.[77]

In ancient civilizations we also find ideas corresponding to the superstitions we have cited. Among the Indics and Greeks we find, for example, the rule not to gaze into one's reflection in the water,[78] since this action will soon result in death.[79] "When one can no longer see his eidolon in a mirror, this is a sign of death."[80] Also, the Greeks considered it a sign of death if one dreamed that he saw his reflection in water.[81] Germanic belief likewise attributed a thanatoptic significance to the reflection in water. If, however, the same phenomenon in a dream is interpreted as a sign of long life, we will take it up not only as a contrary objective, but will also connect it with the meaning of water-dreams as they have to do with birth.[82]

A connection is readily made here with the interesting mythological traditions which demonstrate the belief in the fecundating effect attributed to the shadow in mirror-superstitions as well[83]—primarily the myth of Dionysus and the mysteries re-

74. Warneck, *Lebenskräfte des Evangeliums* (1908), p. 30, n. 3.

75. Wuttke, *op. cit.*, p. 289.

76. J. A. E. Köhler, *Volksbrauch, Aberglauben . . . im Voigtlande* (Leipzig, 1867), p. 423.

77. In Russian superstition, the mirror-image of a person is connected with his innermost being (Spencer [Vetter], *op. cit.*, p. 426).

78. Frazer, "The Belief . . . ," p. 94.

79. Ludwig Preller, *Griechische Mythologie* [4th ed.; Berlin, 1894], I, 598.

80. Hermann Oldenberg, *Die Religion der Veda* (2nd ed.; Stuttgart, 1917), p. 527.

81. Frazer, "The Belief . . . ," p. 94.

82. Haberland, *op. cit.*

83. The following is after Haberland, *op. cit.*, pp. 328 f. The ancient belief reported by Aristotle and Pliny, that a mirror into which a menstruating woman gazes becomes spotted, may be cited here only incidentally.

lating to it. His mother, Persephone, had looked at herself in a
mirror before she bore Zagreus,[84] a fact which Negelein interprets
as a "conception through the coeffectivity of personality and
double." As we know, Zagreus, upon his rebirth as Dionysus,
was carried in Zeus' thigh as a compensation, as it were, for his
original female conception. In this story of rebirth, too, a mirror
has its share. The polymorphous Zagreus was looking at himself
as a bull in a mirror made by Hephaistos, when the Titans sent
by Hera, his enemy, came and tore him apart despite his meta-
morphosis. Only his heart was saved, from which Dionysus was
born in the aforementioned way with the help of Semele.[85] But
Proclus reports one more significant genethliac myth concerning Dionysus: he is said to have looked at himself in the mirror
forged by Hephaistos and, *led astray by this image,* to have
created all things.[86] This late-Greek idea of the creation of the
material world has its archetype in Indic cosmogony, which took
the reflection of the primeval essence to be the foundation of the
material world and which continued in Neo-Platonic and gnostic
doctrines. Thus the gnostics asserted that Adam had lost his di-
vine nature by gazing into a mirror and becoming enamored of
his own reflection.[87]

The harmful effect of contemplating one's reflection in a mirror is clearly represented by the legend of Entelidas, as reported
by Plutarch.[88] Entelidas, delighted by his reflection in the water,
became ill of his own evil gaze and lost his beauty upon recover-
ing health.

The well-known fable of Narcissus in the late version trans-
mitted to us combines in a unique synthesis both aspects of the
belief: the ruinous and the erotic. Ovid relates that at the birth
of Narcissus the seer Tiresias was asked if the child could expect
a long life. The answer was yes, as long as he does not see himself.[89] Once, however, Narcissus, who was equally unresponsive

In Mecklenburg and Silesia mirrors are covered, as in the case of a death,
also when a woman in childbed is in the house, apparently to protect
the child in the womb from enchantments.

84. Georg Friedrich Creuzer, *Symbolik und Mythologie der alten
Völker, besonders der Griechen* (3rd ed.; Leipzig and Darmstadt, 1836–
1843), IV, 196.
85. Wolfgang Menzel, *Die vorchristliche Unsterblichkeitslehre* (Leipzig, 1870 [1869]), II, 66.
86. Menzel, *op. cit.;* Creuzer, *op. cit.,* IV, 129.
87. Menzel, *op. cit.,* p. 68.
88. *Moralia, quest. conv.* V 7, 3.
89. *Metamorphoses* iii. 342 ff.

to youths and maidens, caught sight of himself in the water and became so enamored of the handsome boy so splendidly reflected that the longing for this image caused his death. According to a later legend, Narcissus took his own life after having become entranced by his reflection; and even in the nether world he saw his image in the Styx. According to a still later rationalist view in Pausanias,[90] Narcissus became inconsolable after the death of his twin sister, who resembled him completely in clothing and appearance, until he viewed his reflection; and, although he knew that he saw only his shadow, he still felt a certain assuagement of his affection's grief.[91] Even though we know that the questioning of Tiresias, and other elements,[92] are a later poetic embroidery upon the original legend, it still does not seem to be certain that the fable originally, as Frazer thinks,[93] was only a poetic expression of the superstition that the youth died after viewing his reflection (his double) in the water. Nor is it certain that his falling in love with his own image—which, after all, is the essence of the Narcissus legend—only later developed into an explanation when this original meaning was no longer known.

90. Pausanias 9, 31, 6.
91. A comic counterpart to this is offered by the Kamchatka narrative of the simple god Kutka, on whom the mouse plays a trick by painting on him, while asleep, the face of a woman. When he sees this in the water, he falls in love with himself (Tylor, *op. cit.*, p. 104). Cf. the similar idea of Hebbel [p. 24, note 24].
92. I.e., the union of Narcissus with his echo which, unheard by the coy youth, is consumed with sorrow until "vox tantum atque ossa supersunt" ["only her voice and her bones (lineaments?) survive"]. As punishment for this spurned love, the poet causes the youth to fall into tormenting self-love.
93. Frazer, "The Belief . . . ," p. 94.

V

Narcissism and the Double

> It is the phantom of our own Self,
> whose intimate relationship with, and
> deep effect upon, our spirit casts us
> into hell or transports us into Heaven.
>
> E. T. A. HOFFMANN

By no means can psychoanalysis consider it as a mere accident that the death significance of the double appears closely related to its narcissistic meaning—as also noted elsewhere in Greek legend. Our reason for not being satisfied with Frazer's account lies in the fact that his explanation of the Narcissus fable only shifts the problem to the question of the origin and significance of the underlying superstitious ideas. If we accept the basis of Frazer's assumption and look first for an explanation of why the idea of death in the Narcissus legend, associated with the sight of the double, should have been masked especially by the theme of self-love,[1] then we are compelled next to think of the gener-

---

1. Friedrich Wieseler, *Narkissos* (Göttingen, 1856) conceives of Narcissus as a malign spirit of death (pp. 76 ff.), but also relates the myth to cold egoism (pp. 37, 74).

ally effective tendency to exclude with particular stubbornness the idea of death, which is extremely painful to our self-esteem. To this tendency correspond the frequent euphemistic substitute-ideas, which in superstition gradually come to overlie the original death meaning. In the myth of the Fates, in the changed forms of which the goddess of love takes the place of the goddess of death, Freud has shown that this tendency aims at establishing an equivalent as distant and pleasant as possible—the reason being an understandable endeavor to compensate.[2] This development of the motif, however, is not capricious. It only refers to an old, original identity of these two figures. This identity is consciously based upon the conquest of death by a new procreation and finds its deepest foundation in the relationship to the mother.

That the death meaning of the double likewise tends to be replaced by the love meaning can be seen from manifestly late, secondary, and isolated traditions. According to these traditions, girls are able to see their sweethearts in the mirror under the same conditions in which death or misfortune also reveal themselves.[3] And in the exception that this does not apply to vain girls we may recognize a reference to narcissism, which interferes with the choice of a love object. Similarly, in the Narcissus legend there is a late but psychologically valid version which reports that the handsome youth thought he saw his beloved twin sister (his sweetheart) in the water. Besides this plainly narcissistic infatuation, the death meaning too has so much validity that the close association and deep relationship of both complexes are removed from any doubt.

The Narcissus meaning by its nature is not alien to the motif of the double, which exhibits meanings of the spirit and of death in the folklore material. This observation is shown not simply from the cited mythological traditions of creation by self-reflection, but above all by the literary treatments which cause the Narcissus theme to appear in the forefront along with the problem of death, be it directly or in pathological distortion.

Along with fear and hate of the double, the narcissistic in-

2. S. Freud, "Das Motiv der Kästchenwahl," *Imago*, II (1913), 257–66; [*Gesammelte Schriften* (London, 1949), X, 24–37].

3. Also when the meaning of death, as we have seen, has changed into a general indication of the future, the transition to a meaning of happiness (love, wealth) is easily provided. The wish-fantasies of a promising expectation take the place of an unavoidable gloomy future.

fatuation in one's own image and self is most strongly marked in Oscar Wilde's *Dorian Gray*. "The sense of his own beauty came on him like a revelation" at the first view of his portrait, when he "stood gazing at the shadow of his own loveliness."[4] At the same time, the fear seizes him that he could become old and different— a fear closely associated with the idea of death: "When I find that I am growing old, I shall kill myself" (p. 42). Dorian, who is directly characterized as Narcissus,[5] loves his own image and therefore his own body: "Once, in boyish mockery of Narcissus, he had kissed . . . those painted lips that now smiled so cruelly at him. Morning after morning he had sat before the portrait, wondering at its beauty, almost enamoured of it, as it seemed to him at times" (p. 126). "Often . . . he himself would creep upstairs to the locked room . . . and stand with a mirror in front of the portrait . . . looking now at the evil and aging face on the canvas, and now at the fair young face that laughed back at him from the polished glass. . . . He grew more and more enamoured of his own beauty . . ." (p. 150).

Tied in with this narcissistic attitude is his imposing egoism, his inability to love, and his abnormal sexual life. The intimate friendships with young men, for which Hallward reproaches him, are attempts to realize the erotic infatuation with his own youthful image.[6] From women he is able to obtain only the crudest sensual pleasures, without being capable of a spiritual relation-

4. [Wilde, *op. cit.*, pp. 40–41.]

5. Hallward had previously painted him like this also: "You had leant over the still pool of some Greek woodland, and seen in the water's silent silver the marvel of your own face" [Wilde, *op. cit.*, pp. 135–36.]

6. On the significance of narcissism for the homosexual predilection and its choice of love-object, see my "Beitrag zum Narzissimus," *Jahrbuch für Psychoanalytische und Psychopathologische Forschungen*, III (1912), 401–26, as well as the works of Freud, Sadger, and others, on which it is based. Sadger has already called attention to the relationship of the double to narcissism and to various sexual fantasies; see "Psychiatrisch-Neurologisches in psychoanalytischer Beleuchtung," *Zentralblatt f. d. Gesamtgeb. d. Medizin* (1908), Nos. 7 and 8. A pathologically distinct narcissism is found in the interesting self-observation of a man who likes to talk a great deal with his second self: "Especially in the evening I take a chair and mirror and for almost an hour contemplate my face. . . . Then I lie in bed, take the mirror, smile at myself, and think: what a pity it is that no one sees you now . . . you are a girl, completely so. Then I kiss myself in the mirror; that is, I slowly move the mirror to my lips, gazing at myself therein. In this way, I kiss my second self and admire his good appearance." Also, he calls his second self a "sorry fellow" (*Zentralblatt für Psychoanalyse*, IV [1914], 415).

ship. Dorian shares this defective capacity for love with almost
all double-heroes.[7] He himself says in a significant quotation that
this deficiency arises from his narcissistic fixation on his own ego
" 'I wish I could love,' cried Dorian Gray, with a deep note of

7. It seems a subtle poetic touch when Lenau gives a narcissistic justifica-
tion to the Swedish legend of the connection of the loss of one's
shadow with infertility:

> By the lake stands Anna, dreaming,
> Gazing at the waters bright,
> Sees her beauty at her gleaming,
> Self-reflected, feels delight.

> Speaks: "O beauty of the rarest,
> Wondrous virgin, canst reply,
> Sweden's maids of all the fairest,
> Am I thou? and art thou I?"

> From the lake's green borders bending
> Downward to her image near,
> From her breast her garments rending,
> Anna sees her bosom bare.

> Downward does she gaze, admiring,
> Doubting, blissful, at the sight;
> And the form, herself desiring,
> Stares, transported with delight.

> With the gestures so enraptured,
> Anna sees her beauty grow,
> Which her image now has captured,
> And to her enthralled, doth show.

> "Would that thus I be forever!"
> Cries she, self-enamoured, vain,
> "Would that th'imaged self go never!"
> Hark! the rushing winds bring rain!

> And her likeness now is vanished
> In the foaming water's swirl;
> Like a dream, to nothing banished,
> Sees herself the hapless girl.

Then the old woman appears, and warns her of the danger to her beauty
from bearing children:

> "Oh, then do thy *shadow* query [Rank's emphasis]:
> Art thou mine, ye cheeks so wan?
> These my eyes, so hollow, weary?
> And thou'lt weep into the pond."

She demands of the old woman that her beauty never pass away, and does
enjoy this favor for fully seven years:

> Oft, with bolted door's protection,
> Is she all unseen alone,
> Darts her gaze to her reflection,
> Feasts upon herself so shown.

[See *Lenaus Werke,* ed. C. A. von Bloedau (Leipzig, n.d.), Part I, pp.
315–26.]

pathos in his voice. 'But I seem to have lost the passion, and forgotten the desire. *I am too much concentrated on myself* [Rank's
emphasis]. My own personality has become a burden to me. I
want to escape, to go away, to forget' " (p. 232). In a particularly clear *defensive form, The Student of Prague* shows how the
feared self obstructs the love for a woman; and in Wilde's novel
it becomes clear that fear and hate with respect to the double-self
are closely connected with the narcissistic love for it and with the
resistance of this love. The more Dorian despises his image,
which is becoming old and ugly, the more intensive does his
self-love become: "The very sharpness of the contrast used to
quicken his sense of pleasure. He grew more and more enamoured of his own beauty . . ." (p. 150).

This erotic attitude toward one's own self, however, is only
possible because along with it the defensive feelings can be dis-
charged by way of the hated and feared double. Narcissus is
ambivalent toward his ego for something in him seems to resist
exclusive self-love. The form of defense against narcissicism finds
expression principally in two ways: in fear and revulsion before
one's own image, as seen in Dorian and most of the characters of
Jean Paul; or, as in the majority of cases, in the loss of the
shadow-image or mirror-image.[8] This loss, however, is no loss at

8. What forms the defensive attitude toward the mirrored self can
assume is shown by a trial which took place in 1913 in London. The following is cited from a report of the trial in a daily newspaper (December
9, 1913). A young lord had locked up his beautiful, unfaithful sweetheart for eight days' punishment in a room whose walls consisted of panes of
plate glass. These had the purpose "of constantly offering her countenance
to the young lady so that she might contemplate it, and vow to improve
her ways in the sight of herself. In the course of the days and nights which
the young girl spent partly awake, she felt such a horror of the ever-
recurrent image of her own face that her reason began to be confused.
She continually attempted to avoid the reflection; yet from all sides her
own image grinned and smiled at her. One morning, the old serving-
woman was called in by a terrible rumpus: Miss R. was striking the reflecting walls with both fists; fragments were flying around and into her
face, but she paid no heed to them; she kept on smashing, with only the
purpose of no longer seeing the image of which she had conceived such a
horror. The physician who was called in stated that a frenzy had broken
out in her which probably had become incurable, and attributed the cause
to the solitude in the room, in which the young girl had had nothing to
look at except her mirrored image." The terrible result of this punishment
indicates how greatly she was affected psychologically.

Eduard Fuchs, in the supplementary volume, *The Age of Gallantry*,
of his *Illustrierte Sittengeschichte* (Munich, 1909–1912) states that places
devoted to amorous activities were lavishly provided with mirrors, and he
refers also to the testimony of Casanova. In contrast to the above report,

all, as the persecutions show. On the contrary, it is strengthening, a becoming independent and superiorly strong, which in its turn only shows the exceedingly strong interest in one's own self. Thus the apparent contradiction—the loss of the shadow-image or mirror-image represented as pursuit—is understood as a representation of the opposite, the recurrence of what is repressed in that which represses (see the concluding paragraph of this chapter).

This same mechanism is shown by the dénouement of madness, almost regularly leading to suicide, which is so frequently linked with pursuit by the double, the self. Even when the depiction does not measure up to Dostoyevsky's unsurpassable clinical exactitude, it does become clear that it is a question of paranoid ideas of pursuit and influencing to which the hero is prey by reason of his double. Since Freud's psychoanalytic clarification of paranoia, we know that this illness has as a basis "a fixation in narcissism," to which corresponds typical megalomania, the sexual overrating of oneself.[9] The stage of development from which paranoids regress to their original narcissism is sublimated homosexuality, against the undisguised eruption of which they defend themselves with the characteristic mechanism of projection. On the basis of this insight, it can easily be shown that the pursuit of the ill person regularly proceeds from the originally loved persons (or their surrogates).

The literary representations of the double-motif which describe the persecution complex confirm not only Freud's concept of the narcissistic disposition toward paranoia, but also, in an intuition rarely attained by the mentally ill, they reduce the chief pursuer to the ego itself, the person formerly loved most of all, and now direct their defense against it.[10] This view does not contradict the

the following passage is cited from Fuchs: "She was surprised by the marvel of seeing, without moving, her charming person in a thousand different ways. Her likeness was multiplied by the mirrors—thanks to an ingenious arrangement of the candles—and offered her a new spectacle, from which she was unable to avert her gaze" (ibid., p. 16).

In a variant of the Snow White fairy tale from Rumanian Transylvania, the foster-mother finally is locked up for punishment (of her vanity) in a room, the walls of which consist of nothing but mirrors.—Ernst Böklen, Schneewittchen-Studien [in Mythologische Bibliothek (Leipzig, 1915), Vol. VII, fasc. 3], p. 51.

9. S. Freud, "Psychoanalytische Bemerkungen über einen autobiographisch beschriebenen Fall von Paranoia (Dementia paranoides)," 1911; [see Gesammelte Schriften (London, 1943), VIII, 239–94].

10. The significance of the pursuer's possibly being of the other sex in the picture of paranoia cannot be discussed here. A counterpart to paranoid

homosexual etiology of paranoia. We know, as was already mentioned, that the homosexual love object was originally chosen with a narcissistic attitude toward one's own image.

Connected with paranoid pursuit is yet another theme which deserves emphasis. We know that the person of the pursuer frequently represents the father or his substitute (brother, teacher, etc.), and we also find in our material that the double is often identified with the brother. It is clearest in Musset but also appears in Hoffmann (*The Devil's Elixirs, The Doubles*), Poe, Dostoyevsky, and others. The appearance for the most part is as a twin and reminds us of the legend of the womanish Narcissus, for Narcissus thinks that he sees in his image his sister, who resembles him in every respect. That those writers who preferred the theme of the double also had to contend with the male sibling complex follows from the not infrequent treatment of fraternal rivalry in their other works. So Jean Paul, in the famous novel *The Twins*, has treated the theme of twin brothers who compete with each other, as has Maupassant in *Peter and John* and the unfinished novel *The Angelus*, Dostoyevsky in *The Brothers Karamasov*, and so on.[11]

Actually, and considered externally, the double is the rival of his prototype in anything and everything, but primarily in the love for woman—a trait which he may partly owe to the identification with the brother. One author expresses himself about this relationship in another connection: "The younger brother is accustomed, even in ordinary life, to be somehow similar to the elder, at least in external appearance. He is, as it were, a reflection of his fraternal self which has come to life; and on this account he is also a rival in everything that the brother sees, feels, and thinks."[12] What connection this identification might have

---

illness as a consequence of defending narcissism is shown by Raimund's presentation of Rappelkopf's cure of his paranoid delusion by deliberately introducing the double. Also, Rappelkopf's ideas of being influenced proceed primarily from his wife, by whom he feels persecuted and from whom he flees in order "tenderly to make a wife" of solitude. But here the author succeeds in reversing the projection: instead of loving herself and hating others, the hero learns to love others and to hate himself.

11. Besides these, cf. the play *Brüder* (1902) by J. E. Poritzky, the author of several stories of the double; cf. also the play of the same title by Paul Lindau (after the novel by the same author), who likewise gave particular interest to the theme of the double. The comedy of mixed identities based on the motif of twins permits the humorous resolution of tragic fraternal rivalry.

12. J. B. Schneider, "Das Geschwisterproblem," *Geschlecht und Gesellschaft*, VIII (1913), 381.

with the narcissistic attitude may be shown by another statement by the same author: "The relationship of the older to the younger brother is analogous to that of the masturbator to himself."

From this fraternal attitude of rivalry toward the hated competitor in the love for the mother, the death wish and the impulse toward murder against the double becomes reasonably understandable,[13] even though the significance of the brother in this case does not exhaust our understanding. The theme of the brothers is not precisely the root of the belief in the double, but rather only an interpretation—well-determined, to be sure—of the doubtlessly purely subjective meaning of the double. This meaning is not sufficiently explained by the psychological statement that "the mental conflict creates the double," which corresponds to a "projection of inner turmoil" and the shaping of which brings about an inner liberation, an unburdening, even if at the price of the "fear of encounter." So "fear shapes from the ego-complex the terrifying phantom of the double," which "fulfills the secret, always suppressed wishes of his soul."[14] Only after determining this formal meaning of the double do the real problems arise, for we aim at an understanding of the psychological situation and of the attitude which together create such an inner division and projection.

The most prominent symptom of the forms which the double takes is a powerful consciousness of guilt which forces the hero no longer to accept the responsibility for certain actions of his ego, but to place it upon another ego, a double, who is either personified by the devil himself[15] or is created by making a diabolical pact. This detached personification of instincts and desires which were once felt to be unacceptable, but which can be satisfied without responsibility in this indirect way, appears in other forms of the theme as a beneficent admonitor (e.g., *William Wilson*) who is directly addressed as the "conscience" of the person (e.g., Dorian Gray, etc.). As Freud has demonstrated, this

13. So also does the sympathy which makes of the rival a sort of protective spirit (*William Wilson*), or even a person who sacrifices himself for the welfare of his double—e.g., as in Dickens' *Tale of Two Cities,* in which the doubles love the same girl (rivalry), and one of them permits himself to be executed for the other. In this way, the original death wish, even though in altered form, is realized, after all, by the elimination of the rival.

14. Emil Lucka, "Dostojewski und der Teufel," *Literarisches Echo,* XVI (December 15, 1913), 6.

15. Dostoyevsky's *The Brothers Karamasov,* Jean Paul's *Confession,* or in *Satan's Memoirs,* cited by Sadger, *op. cit.*

awareness of guilt, having various sources, measures on the one hand the distance between the ego-ideal and the attained reality; on the other, it is nourished by a powerful fear of death and creates strong tendencies toward self-punishment, which also imply suicide.[16]

After having stressed the narcissistic significance of the double in its positive meaning as well as in its various defensive forms, it still remains for us to understand more about the meaning of death in our material and to demonstrate its relationship to the meaning already gained. What the folkloric representations and several of the literary ones directly reveal is a tremendous thanatophobia, which refers to the defensive symptoms heretofore discussed to the extent that, in these, fear (of the image, of its loss, or of pursuit) formed the most prominent characteristic.

One motif which reveals a certain connection between the fear of death and the narcissistic attitude is the wish to remain forever young. On the one hand, this wish represents the libidinous fixation of the individual onto a definite developmental stage of the ego; and on the other, it expresses the fear of becoming old, a fear which is really the fear of death.[17] Thus Wilde's Dorian says, "When I find that I am growing old, I shall kill myself" (p. 42). Here we are at the significant theme of suicide, at which point a whole series of characters come to their ends while pursued by their doubles. Of this motif, apparently in such contradiction to the asserted fear of death, it can be shown precisely from its special application in this connection that it is closely relevant not only to the theme of thanatophobia, but also with narcissism. For these characters and their creators—as far as they attempted suicide or did carry it out (Raimund, Maupassant)—did not fear death; rather, the *expectation* of the unavoidable destiny of death is unbearable to them. As Dorian Gray expresses it: "I have no terror of Death. It is only *the coming* [Rank's emphasis] of Death that terrifies me" (p. 231). The normally unconscious thought of the approaching destruction of the self—the most general example of the repression of an unen-

16. S. Freud, "Zur Einführung des Narzissmus," 1914; [see *Gesammelte Schriften* (London, 1946), X, 137–70].

17. Cf. Adolf Wilbrandt's [*Der*] *Meister von Palmyra* [Stuttgart, 1889] for a representation of this theme, which has an interesting relationship to the love for a woman. [Cf. also Th. C. van Stockum, "Ein vergessenes deutsches Drama: Adolf Wilbrandts *Der Meister von Palmyra*," in *Von Friedrich Nicolai bis Thomas Mann: Aufsätze zur deutschen und vergleichenden Literaturgeschichte* (Groningen, 1961), pp. 254–73.]

durable certainty—torments these unfortunates with the conscious idea of their eternal, eternal [*sic*] inability to return, an idea from which release is only possible in death. Thus we have the strange paradox of the suicide who voluntarily seeks death in order to free himself of the intolerable thanatophobia.

It could be objected that the fear of death is simply the expression of an overly strong instinct for self-preservation, insisting upon fulfillment. Certainly the only too-justified fear of death, seen as one of the fundamental evils of mankind, has its main root in the self-preservation instinct, the greatest threat to which is death. But this motivation is insufficient for pathological thanatophobia, which occasionally leads directly to suicide. In this neurotic constellation—in which the material to be repressed and against which the individual defends himself is finally and actually realized—it is a question of a complicated conflict in which, along with the ego-instincts serving self-preservation, the libidinous tendencies also function, which are merely rationalized in the conscious ideas of fear. Their unconscious participation explains fully the pathological fear arising here, behind which we must expect a portion of repressed libido. This, along with other already-known factors,[18] we believe we have found in that part of narcissism which feels just as intensely threatened by the idea of death as do the pure ego-instincts, and which thereupon reacts with the pathological fear of death and its final consequences.

As proof that the pure ego-interests of self-preservation cannot explain the pathological fear of death satisfactorily to other observers either, we cite the testimony of a researcher who is completely unprejudiced psychologically. Spiess, from whose work we have borrowed many a documentation, expresses the view that "man's horror of death does not result merely from the natural love of life." He explains this with the following words:

That, however, is not a dependency upon earthly existence, for man often hates that. . . . No, it is the love for the personality peculiar to him, found in his conscious possession, the love for his self, for the central self of his individuality, which attaches him to life. This *self-love* is an inseparable element of his being. In it is

18. The defense against death wishes, originating in the libido (jealousy), toward closely related competitors (e.g., a brother) takes the form of turning against oneself (self-punishment). In a case of severe attacks of thanatophobia, the intermediate stage of death wishes directed against closely related persons could easily be demonstrated: the patient declares that these severe fears of death first applied to those members of his family nearest to him (mother, brother) before they attacked himself.

founded and rooted the instinct for self-preservation, and from it emerges the deep and powerful longing to escape death or the submergence into nothingness, and the hope of again awakening to a new life and to a new era of continuing development.[19] The thought of losing oneself is so unbearable for man, and it is this thought which makes death so terrible for him. . . . This hopeful longing may be criticized as childish vanity, foolish megalomania; the fact remains that it lives in our hearts; it influences and rules over our imagination and endeavors (p. 115).

This relationship is evident in all of its desirable clarity—indeed, downright plasticity—in literary material, although narcissistic self-assertion and self-exaggeration generally prevail there. The frequent slaying of the double, through which the hero seeks to protect himself permanently from the pursuits of his self, is really a suicidal act. It is, to be sure, in the painless form of slaying a different ego: an unconscious illusion of the splitting-off of a bad, culpable ego—a separation which, moreover, appears to be the precondition for every suicide. The suicidal person is unable to eliminate by direct self-destruction the fear of death resulting from the threat to his narcissism. To be sure, he seizes upon the only possible way out, suicide, but he is incapable of

19. Here, taphephobia may be recalled, which Poe, Dostoyevsky, and other writers reveal. Merezhkovsky has shown this pathological fear of death to be the most important factor for the understanding of Tolstoy's transformation and personality; see *Tolstoi und Dostojewski*, tr. Carl von Gütschow (Leipzig, 1903), pp. 27 f. Toward the close of the 1870's such an "onset of the fear of death," according to Merezhkovsky, "almost drove him to suicide" (p. 30). Merezhkovsky finds the source of this overwhelming fear of death logically in its reverse aspect—a strong love of life, manifested in the form of a boundless love for his body. He does not tire of emphasizing this love for his own self as being Tolstoy's most essential trait of character, even from the dim memory of his earliest childhood. Tolstoy mentions a bath when he was three or four years old as one of his happiest impressions: "For the first time I caught sight of my small body with the ribs visible on my chest, and grew fond of it." Merezhkovsky establishes that from this moment on, this attitude toward his body never left him for the remainder of his life (pp. 52 f.). Of Tolstoy's activity as a teacher, Merezhkovsky says: "An eternal Narcissus, he took pleasure in the reflection of his ego in the minds of the children. . . . In the children, too, he loved . . . only himself, himself alone" (p. 15). As a counterpart to Jean Paul's well-defined fear of seeing his own limbs, and as one example of several, we may refer to the passage in *Anna Karenina* where Vronsky complacently observes his "elastic calf," which he injured shortly before: "Earlier, too, he had felt the joyful awareness of his physical life, but never before had he loved himself—his body—so much" (p. 53). "The love of oneself—everything begins and ends with this. Love or hate of oneself, only of oneself: these are the principal and only hubs—now apparent, now concealed—around which everything turns and moves in the first and perhaps most honest works of L. Tolstoy" (p. 12).

carrying it out other than by way of the phantom of a feared and hated double, because he loves and esteems his ego too highly to give it pain or to transform the idea of his destruction into the deed.[20] In this subjective meaning, the double turns out to be a functional expression of the psychological fact that an individual with an attitude of this kind cannot free himself from a certain phase of his narcissistically loved ego-development. He encounters it always and everywhere, and it constrains his actions within a definite direction. Here, the allegorical interpretation of the double as a part of the ineradicable past gets its psychological meaning. What attaches the person to the past becomes clear, and why this assumes the form of the double is evident.[21]

20. The narcissistic element of forbearance in the suicide of the double is shown very nicely by Gautier in the duelling scene of his already-mentioned short story *The Exchange of Souls:* "Each one actually had his own body before him and was compelled to plunge the steel into flesh which still had belonged to him two days previously. The duel developed into a kind of unforeseen suicide; and although Octave and the Count were both brave, they felt an instinctive terror when, with daggers in their hands, they found themselves facing their own selves, ready to attack each other" (p. 136). Such a situation is also indicated in Arthur Schnitzler's short story *Casanova's Homecoming*, in which Casanova, slipping away in the dawn from a purchased night of love, is challenged by his young twin and rival with whom, from the first moment, he feels strangely congenial. Casanova has thrown nothing but a coat around his naked body and, so that he be at no disadvantage confronting his opponent, the latter undressed also. "Lorenzi stood opposite him, as splendidly naked as a young god. 'If I should cast down my dagger,' thought Casanova. 'If I embraced him?'"

Similarly, the writer creates for himself even in the main character a double whom he allows to die for himself. In primitive form this is evident in the well-known stories of the double life of one and the same person—e.g., in Stevenson's *The Strange Case of Doctor Jekyll and Mr. Hyde;* H. G. Wells' *Love and Mr. Lewisham;* Kipling's *At the End of the Passage,* and Wiedmann's *A Double Life.* With these are associated the related descriptions of [August Hoffmann von] Vestenhof's *The Man with the Three Eyes* [Munich, 1913] (a dual existence in one body) and the last book of the elder Rosny [J. Henri], *The Enigma of Givreuse,* which treats the duplication of one person (scientifically) and combines this with the rivalry of the two doubles for one girl. Most recently, the theme of the double has again been brought to the stage in George Kaiser's symbolic play *The Coral*, in which the multimillionaire flees into the soul of his double, his secretary, in order to partake of the latter's blissful childhood and guiltlessness. He murders the secretary and assumes his identity, although he is then considered to be the murderer of the multimillionaire and can prove his true identity only by means of the coral.

21. In his fragmentary work *Funeral Rites* (*Dziady*, 1823–32), Adam B. Mickiewicz has dealt with the problem of the double by having the suicide Gustav awaken at the moment of his death to a new, second life.

Finally, the significance of the double as an embodiment of the soul—a notion represented in primitive belief and living on in our superstition—has close relevance to the previously discussed factors. It seems that the development of the primitive belief in the soul is largely analogous to the psychological circumstances demonstrated here by the pathological material—an observation which would seem to confirm anew the "agreement in the psychology of aborigines and of neurotics." This circumstance would also explain how the primitive conditions are repeated in the later mythical and artistic representations of the theme, specifically with particular emphasis on the libidinous factors which do not so clearly emerge in the primeval history but which nonetheless allowed us to form a conclusion about the less transparent primal phenomena.

Freud, by pointing out the animistic view of the world based on the power of thoughts, has justified our thinking of primitive man, just as of the child,[22] as being exquisitely narcissis-

---

In this new life he really experiences his first life up to the point of death, since he cannot live beyond this definite point (kind communication from Dr. [Paul?] Federn). We find this psychological mechanism typified in a *literal* way, from our point of view, in the song of the petrified youth, sung by a child as an interlude. Once a knight, von Twardow, takes an old castle by assault and finds, in a closed vault, a young man in chains standing before a mirror; little by little he is turning to stone through a magic spell. In the course of two centuries he is already petrified up to his chest; yet his face is still youthful and lively! The knight, knowing of the spell, is about to shatter the mirror, thereby liberating the youth, but the latter wishes to have the mirror in order to release himself from the curse:

> Took it, and sighed—and paling, he gazes
> Into it with weeping and moan:
> And then for a kiss the mirror he raises—
> And turned all into stone.

(See *Totenfeier*, translated into German by Siegfried Lipiner [Leipzig, 1887], p. 9.)

22. See Fritz Wittels, "Das Ich des Kindes," in *Die sexuelle Not* (Vienna, 1909), p. 109. Here Wittels describes very charmingly the awakening of the child's awareness of himself and its connection with egotism: "When I was still a small boy, I woke up one day with the overwhelming realization that I was an 'I,' that I looked externally, to be sure, like other children but nonetheless was fundamentally different and tremendously more important. I stood before the mirror, observed myself attentively, and often repeatedly addressed my image by my first name. In doing so, I evidently intended to create a bridge from the image in the external world over to me, across which I might penetrate into my unfathomable self. I do not know if I kissed my reflection, but I have seen other children kissing theirs: they come to terms with their ego by loving it." While correcting proof, I see by chance the last book of this author,

tic.[23] Also, the narcissistic theories of the creation of the world which he cites, just like the later philosophical systems based on the ego (e.g., Fichte), indicate that man is able to perceive the reality surrounding him mainly only as a reflection, or as a part, of his ego.[24] Likewise, Freud [see n. 23] has pointed out that it is death, ANANKE the implacable, which opposes the primitive man's narcissism and obliges him to turn over a part of his omnipotence to the spirits. Linked to this fact of death, however, which is forced upon man and which he constantly seeks to deny, are the first concepts of the soul, which can be traced in primitive peoples as well as those of advanced cultures.

Among the very first and most primitive concepts of the soul is that of the shadow, which appears as a faithful image of the body but of a lighter substance. It is true that Wundt contends that the shadow provided an original motif for the concept of the soul.[25] He believes that the "shadow-soul," the *alter ego*, as distinct from that of the body, "as far as we can tell has its sole source in dreams and visions."[26] But other researchers—Tylor, for example—have shown by a wealth of material that among primitive peoples designations of images or shadows predominate;[27] and Heinzelmann, who finds support in the most recent investigations, objects to Wundt on this point by showing in an abundance of examples "that here, too, it is a question of quite constant and extensively recurring views (*loc. cit.*, p. 19 [*sic*]). Just as Spencer justly asserts in the case of the child,[28] primitive man considers his shadow as something real, as a being attached

---

Über den Tod . . . (Vienna, 1914), which reduces the problem of death to that of the fear of death [cf. Rank's "The Double As Immortal Self"].

23. S. Freud, "Animismus, Magie und Allmacht der Gedanken," *Imago*, II (1913), 1–21 [this is the title of the third part of the paper "Über einige Übereinstimmungen im Seelenleben der Wilden und der Neurotiker"].

24. Cf. J. Frazer, "The Belief . . . ," p. 19. "He is a boundless egoist," says Heinzelmann (*op. cit.*, p. 14), after H. Visscher, *Religion und soziales Leben bei den Naturvölkern* (Bonn, 1911), I, 117; II, 243 ff.

25. W. M. Wundt, *Völkerpsychologie* . . . [4th ed.; Stuttgart, 1912], Vol. II, Part 2.

26. For emphasis placed upon the dream as the main source for the belief in the survival of the soul after death, see Frazer, "The Belief . . . ," pp. 57, 140, 214; see also Radestock, *op. cit.*, p. 251. It should not be forgotten that one sees oneself in dreams.

27. E. B. Tylor, *The Beginnings of Culture* [*Primitive Culture?* (3rd ed.; London, 1891)], I, 43 ff.

28. Cf. also the above-cited poem by Stevenson-Dehmel.

to him, and he is confirmed in his view of it as a soul by the
fact that the dead person (who is lying down) simply no longer
casts a shadow.[29] From the experience of dreaming, man may
have taken the proof for his belief that the viable ego might
exist even after death; but only his shadow and his reflected image could have convinced him that he had a mysterious double
even while he was alive.

The various taboos, precautions, and evasions which primitive
man uses with regard to his shadow show equally well his narcissistic esteem of his ego and his tremendous fear of its being
threatened. Primitive narcissism feels itself primarily threatened
by the ineluctable destruction of the self. Very clear evidence of
the truth of this observation is shown by the choice, as the most
primitive concept of the soul, of an image as closely similar as
possible to the physical self, hence a true double. The idea of
death, therefore, is denied by a duplication of the self incor-
porated in the shadow or in the reflected image.

We have seen that among primitives the designations for
shadow, reflected image, and the like, also serve for the notion
"soul," and that the most primitive concept of the soul of the
Greeks, Egyptians, and other culturally prominent peoples coincides with a double which is essentially identical with the body.[30]
Then, too, the concept of the soul as a reflected image assumes
that it resemble an exact copy of the body. Indeed, Negelein
speaks directly of a "primitive monism of body and soul," by
which he means that the idea of the soul originally coincided
completely with that of a second body. As proof he cites the fact
that the Egyptians made images of the dead in order to protect
them from eternal destruction.[31] Such a material origin, then,

29. See Herbert Spencer, *Prinzipien der Soziologie*, tr. into German by
B. Vetter [Stuttgart, 1877–1897], II, 426; see also J. v. Negelein, "Ein
Beitrag zum indischen Seelenwanderungsglauben," in *Arch. f. Rel.-Wiss.*,
1901.

30. According to Rohde, the primary concept of the soul leads to a
duplication of the person, to the formation of a second self. "The soul
which has disappeared at death is the exact copy of the person here
below" (Heinzelmann, *op. cit.*, p. 20). I can add to these citations a
reference to the book by Rudolf Kleinpaul, *Volkspsychologie* (Berlin,
1914), which also gives evidence of a double as the most primitive concept of the soul (pp. 5 f., 131, 171).

31. Cf. mirrors as burial-gifts in the oldest Grecian times (G. F. Creuzer,
op. cit., IV, 196), and among the Mohammedans (K. Haberland, *op.
cit.*).

does the idea of the soul have. Later, it became an immaterial concept with the increasing reality-experience of man, who does not want to admit that death is everlasting annihilation.

Originally, to be sure, the question of a belief in immortality was of no concern; but the complete ignorance of the idea of death arises from primitive narcissism, as it is evidenced even in the child. For the primitive, as for the child, it is self-evident that he will continue to live,[32] and death is conceived of as an unnatural, magically produced event.[33] Only with the acknowledgment of the idea of death, and of the fear of death consequent upon threatened narcissism, does the wish for immortality as such appear. This wish really restores the original naive belief in an eternally continuing existence in partial accommodation to the experience of death gained in the meantime. In this way, therefore, the primitive belief in souls is originally nothing else than a kind of belief in immortality which energetically denies the power of death;[34] and even today the essential content of the belief in the soul—as it subsists in religion, superstition, and modern cults—has not become other, nor much more, than that.[35]

32. Frazer, "The Belief . . . ," pp. 33, 35, 53, and *passim*. Characteristic of this naive view is the remark of the anthropologist K. von den Steinen, who gave a Bakairi-Indian the sentence, "All men must die," to translate into the latter's language. To his great amazement, it turned out that the man was unable to grasp the meaning of this sentence, since he had no idea of the necessity of death (*Unter den Naturvölkern Zentral-Brasiliens* [Berlin, 1894], pp. 344, 348; according to Frazer, "The Belief . . . ," p. 35).

33. Frazer [?], *op. cit.*, pp. 84 ff.

34. Primitive man, in fact, does not know any belief in immortality in our sense. Also, many primitive peoples think of the shadowy life of the mind as gradually fading away, significantly often simultaneously with the body's decomposition; or else they have the view that man dies several times in the underworld until he is finally and definitively dead. This idea agrees largely with the infantile attitude, which lacks the concept of "being dead" in our sense and which considers it to be a matter of passing away by degrees (cf. the corresponding communications under the heading "Kinderseele" in *Imago*).

35. This belief is shown best by the current spiritism, which maintains that the souls of deceased persons return in their human form (spirit), and by the occult meaning of the double. According to this meaning, the soul leaves the body and takes on a material form which becomes visible under favorable conditions (exteriorization of the soul). It appears, further, that the soul originally was identified with the consciousness of oneself which passes away in death. Our modern scientific way of looking at the world has not yet rid itself of this idea, as the affective resistance to accepting a psychology of the unconscious teaches us. The Belgian writer M. Maeter-

The thought of death is rendered supportable by assuring oneself of a second life, after this one, as a double. As in the threat
to narcissism by sexual love, so in the threat of death does the
idea of death (originally averted by the double) recur in this
figure who, according to general superstition, announces death
or whose injury harms the individual.[36]

So, then, we see primitive narcissism as that in which the libidinous interests and those serving self-preservation are concentrated upon the ego with equal intensity, and which in the same
way protect against a series of threats by reactions directed
against the complete annihilation of the ego, or else toward its
damage and impairment. These reactions do not result merely
from the real fear which, as Visscher says, can be termed the defensive form of an exceedingly strong instinct for self-preservation. They arise also from the fact that the primitive, along with
the neurotic, exhibits this "normal" fear, increased to a pathological degree, which "cannot be explained from the actual experiences of terror."[37] We have derived the libidinous component,
which plays a part here, from the equally-intensively felt threat
to narcissism, which resists the utter immolation of the ego just as
much as it resists its dissolution in sexual love. That it is actually
primitive narcissism which resists the threat is shown quite
clearly by the reactions in which we see the threatened narcissism assert itself with heightened intensity: whether it be in the
form of pathological self-love as in Greek legend or in Oscar
Wilde, the representative of the modern esthete; or in the defensive form of the pathological fear of one's self, often leading

---

linck has followed up these problems, merely touched upon here, to the
outermost limits of imaginability in a profound book, *Concerning Death*
(translated into German by F. von Oppeln-Bronikowski [Jena, 1913]).

36. Turgeniev writes to a friend: "Love is one of the passions which
destroy our own egos" (after Merezhkovsky, *op. cit.*, p. 65). How the
male's narcissism seeks to come to terms with this problem is indicated
by a passage, typical of Strindberg's whole attitude toward woman, from
Legends: "We begin to love a woman by depositing with her our souls,
bit by bit. We duplicate our personality; and the beloved woman who
formerly was indifferent and neutral begins to assume the guise of our
other self, becoming our double" (p. 293). In Villiers de l'Isle-Adam's
short story *Vera*, the husband is satisfied to hallucinate his young deceased
wife—to incorporate her, as it were, in his own individuality, and he feels
happy in this duple life. There are narcissistic fantasies and mirror-fantasies
in the same author's short story *Be a Man*.

37. G. Heinzelmann, *op. cit.*, p. 60.

to paranoid insanity and appearing personified in the pursuing shadow, mirror-image, or double. On the other hand, in the same phenomena of defense the threat also recurs, against which the individual wants to protect and assert himself. So it happens that the double, who personifies narcissistic self-love, becomes an unequivocal rival in sexual love; or else, originally created as a wish-defense against a dreaded eternal destruction, he reappears in superstition as the messenger of death.[38]

38. This fundamental trait of the double-problem is further clarified in Freud's essay "Das Unheimliche," 1919; [see *Gesammelte Schriften* (London, 1947), XII, 227–68].

INDEX

(*Fictional characters may be found under the names of their authors.*)